And All That
JAZZ

Colin King

Acknowledgments:

Courtesy of Redferns Music Picture Library:

(Glen A. Baker) p.60; (Max Jones Files) p.6-7, 9, 14-15, 16-17, 18, 21, 22, 23, 24-25 and 95; (Michael Ochs Archive)p.11, 13, 19, 20, 34, 36-37, 39, 43, 45, 47, 49, 51, 54-55, 57, 67, 71, 73, 81, 85, 93 and 96; (William P. Gottlieb) p.3, 27, 30-31, 35, 40, 61, 63, 65 and 69; (David Redfern) p.33, 59, 75, 77, 79, 82-83, 91, 99, 103, 105, 107, 109, 110-111, 115 and 120-121; (Derek Boulton) p.52-53; (Rogan Coles) p.87; (Andrew Putler) p.89 and 113; (Ebert Roberts) p.117; (Tim Hall) p.118; (John Kirk) p.119; (Dave Bennett) p.28

Published in 2003 by Caxton Editions
20 Bloomsbury Street
London WC1B 3JH
a member of the Caxton Publishing Group

Designed and produced for Caxton Editions
by Open Door Limited
Langham, Rutland
Editing: Mary Morton
Colour separation: GA Graphics, Stamford, UK

Title: And All That JAZZ
ISBN: 1 84067 475 X

And All That
JAZZ

Colin King

CAXTON EDITIONS

CONTENTS

INTRODUCTION

In this book we examine the early history of jazz from its origins in Africa and watch as it evolves into the variations it has taken to the present day. We will follow the various styles as they appear and look at the major players who kept the pulse of jazz beating.

What is jazz? "Jazz, like any artistic phenomenon, represents the sum of an addition. The factors of this addition are, to my mind, African music, French and American music and folklore" (Robert Goffin 1934).

From its early origins in the Yoruba drumming of West Africa, to its blending with the European folk melodies in America, through the slave trade, through the bootlegger clubs of the Roaring Twenties and to the present day, jazz has been around the world, keeping the rhythms and melodies flowing and people's feet tapping.

The term "jazz" was originally an African-American slang term for the sexual act. It is believed to have arisen in the brothels of New Orleans in the late 19th century, and it is in New Orleans that jazz music was born. From there it moved up the Mississippi river to Memphis, St Louis and finally to Chicago. Jazz started as an American phenomenon but is now an international one.

Early jazz spanned many musical forms such as spirituals, cakewalks, the music of jig bands, ragtime and the blues. Around 1891, Buddy Bolden, a New Orleans barber, is reputed to have picked up his cornet and blown the first stammering notes of jazz, thereby breathing life into a whole new music tradition. In the 1950s jazz, the USA's greatest contribution to music, crossed the threshold of academic circles and became seriously, even religiously, revered.

Jazz now functions as a popular expressive art form and has enjoyed periods of widespread public response. We will follow jazz from its early beginnings, through the hot jazz age of the Roaring Twenties,

the swing era of the late 30s and its peak of popularity in the cool jazz of the late 50s and early 60s. Finally, we will examine jazz as it has evolved up to the present day, both in America, and in the UK.

The history of jazz is essentially a history of people, particularly African American people, without whom there would be no jazz. The book also gives the biographies of many of the major proponents of the genre.

Above: The New Orleans barber, Buddy Bolden (on cornet) and his band.

EARLY JAZZ ERA (1850-1910)

Pre-Jazz

Sadly, much of the early history of jazz has been lost because written records were not kept and recording technology was unavailable. Much of what is known has been learned by working backwards and examining the writings that were available on other subjects surrounding it.

We do know that jazz came about as a blending of cultures in North America. It was the folk music of both the European immigrants and the recently freed African slaves that gave rise to jazz in the late 1800s. European music was complex at this time, for example the operas of Wagner, but the ordinary people of America had simpler tastes. Their popular music was based on what is known as the AABA theme and these simple harmonies and rhythms were played by the masses, particularly in their churches. The African-American slave culture had also developed its own sound in plantation work songs, shouts and spirituals that had evolved from the Yoruba rhythms of West Africa. It is because of this mix of cultures that jazz has inherent in it the polyrhythms and the tonal quality of the human voice. The notes that jazz musicians play are "blue", and are difficult to precisely notate using Western musical scales as these often fall between notes.

A music theme is where a letter is assigned to each theme to indicate the sequence of the form the music takes.

Early Jazz

Early jazz, dating from the late teens to the early 1920s, is pretty much wholly associated with the city of New Orleans. New Orleans is a thriving port with access to the vibrancy of both the Latin culture of Mexico and the African culture of the Caribbean and is, therefore, a cultural melting pot. In the 19th century the city was divided into two areas: downtown with a white and Creole population and uptown with a large African-American population who had only recently been freed from slavery. Most of the white and many of the Creole musicians had been formally trained. However, in 1894, stricter segregation rules were enforced which extended into the venues. This at first forced the Creoles into competition with the largely untrained black musicians, but later this cultural combination meant that they were able to teach the black players, and each side expanded their musical horizons through exchange of ideas.

Music was everywhere in New Orleans. At that time funerals typically featured marching brass bands consisting of trombones, trumpets and the recently invented saxophone. There were also many society dances at which musicians could hone their skills. A 38-square block area had been created by the council which was known as Storyville. Its numerous clubs and brothels, all featuring music and dancing, meant there was ample opportunity for musicians to perform. This mix of ethnicity and opportunity was the perfect breeding ground for the birth of jazz and many famous artists emerged from this exciting city to take jazz to the world.

There is debate as to the exact etymology of the word jazz, and whether it was a Creole or African word in origin. However, it was most certainly used as a slang term or vulgar expression for the sexual act and it is because of the music's early association with the brothels of Storyville that it came to be referred to as "jazz".

There is also debate as to who was the first to "invent" or first play the notes of jazz music. Some say it was Buddy Bolden with his cornet in 1891. However, Jelly Roll Morton claimed that he invented it in 1897, although he did acknowledge Bolden. Certainly, both were influential, so perhaps it is best they share the title of inventor.

Above: Music was everywhere in New Orleans. At that time funerals typically featured marching brass bands consisting of trombones, trumpets and the recently invented saxophone.

BIOGRAPHY:

Jelly Roll Morton

Piano

Jelly Roll Morton is widely regarded as the first jazz composer and arranger. He was born in New Orleans on 20 September 1885 as Ferdinand Lamothe and was of Creole extraction. In 1904 he began his musical career by playing piano in the local brothels. Always a character, he coined his name after he saw an Afro-American vaudeville comedian announce himself as "Sweet Papa Cream Puff, right out of the bakery shop". In the street slang of New Orleans, words such as cream puff and jelly roll were common euphemisms for the genitals and intercourse and so Morton began to modestly announce himself as "Papa Jelly Roll, with stove pipes in my hips and all the women in town dyin' to turn my damper down". Since earning a living as a pianist was so hard, Morton supplemented his income by pimping and hustling, card-sharking, bellhopping and tailoring. Nevertheless, he was an extraordinary performer and he composed pieces such as "New Orleans Blues" and "Jelly Roll Blues" in the early 1900s.

In 1908 he left New Orleans and toured around the Gulf of Mexico coast and the state of Texas. He also went to St Louis where he met with Scott Joplin. In 1917, following a brief tour with a minstrel show, he went to live in California. It was through these travels that he acquired a Latin feel to some of his music, which he was never to lose.

It was Morton who, around 1920, introduced "chord symbols" which acted as an alternative form of musical notation for musicians who had not been formally trained in music, thereby opening up jazz to a whole new group of people.

In 1922 he was established as a musician, arranger, songwriter and bandleader of his Red Hot Peppers Orchestra and he moved to Chicago later that year. Indeed the Peppers' Chicago recording sessions of 1926 and 1927 are thought, by aficionados, to be the best and finest representations of the New Orleans jazz sound. It was here in Chicago that Morton began making money by selling his compositions via sheet music, his first being the hit "Wolverine Blues". Sadly, this prosperity was not to last as the Great Depression hit the entire country. Furthermore, with the introduction of swing, Morton's sound fell out of favour with the general public. Although many of his compositions were still being played, the royalties he was due were being skimmed off by his publisher and Morton found himself upon hard times.

In 1938, after living in relative obscurity for several years, he recorded his *Morton Monologues* which remain as a legacy to the early history of jazz. His health deteriorated and in July 1941 he passed away whilst in Los Angeles.

Above: Jelly Roll Morton (seated) – self-proclaimed inventor of jazz.

RAGTIME

One of the earliest forms of jazz was ragtime. It was in 1895 that Ben Harney published the first ragtime tune. In 1897 "The Mississippi Rag" was published by William Krell, followed by Tom Turpin's composition of "The Harlem Rag" later that year.

The sound of ragtime evolved from jig band music and the music for the cakewalk dance which was all the rage at that time.

The cakewalk was an Afro-American elegant and stylised dance parodying the Caribbean and Southern "white" plantation owners' courtly manners. Sadly there are no cakewalk recordings in existence.

Ragtime utilised the waltzes, marches and polkas of the European tradition but added the syncopation of Afro-American rhythms. It was played in a fast and shallow manner, on specially prepared pianos that reverberated with a jangling sound. Although initially played by solo pianists in bars in the USA, its popularity soon soared and it became a phenomenon all around the world. By the 1900s, recordings were being made by military bands, orchestras and piano/banjo duets. A number of composers wrote in the ragtime form, including James Scott, Louis Chauvin, Joseph Lamb and the man considered to be its founding father, Scott Joplin.

BIOGRAPHY:
Scott Joplin

Piano

Scott Joplin was born in 1868 in Texas. In the 1890s he played cornet in Missouri bands, even making an appearance at the World Fair in 1893. He pioneered ragtime as a serious and elegant musical form.

His first ragtime composition was "The Maple Leaf Rag", named after a club. It was bought in 1899 by John Stark, who was to become Joplin's music publisher. Joplin received royalties in the deal for the song which was fortunate because it became a huge hit on an international level.

He went on to compose many more big-selling songs including "Easy Winner", "Solace" and "The Entertainer" which is still well known today because of its use in the film *The Sting*.

In 1907 Joplin moved to New York where, amongst other works, he composed a ragtime opera called "Treemonisha" and the song "Wall Street Rag". Sadly he had contracted syphilis which was to lead to progressive deterioration in his health, even making it difficult for him to play his beloved cornet. On 1 April 1917 Joplin died in a Manhattan hospital.

Whilst it can be argued that Joplin's compositions go against the improvisational nature of jazz, his influence was immense upon many of the musicians that we associate with jazz today. He even influenced the likes of Stravinsky and Debussy with his syncopated and ragged rhythms and his musical compositions continue to be played.

New Orleans certainly played an important role in the origins of jazz at the turn of the 20th century, but there seem to have been similar developments taking place in many other cities in the States where there were large African-American populations. Kansas City, Chicago and St Louis were all major areas where jazz music evolved.

Above: Scott Joplin – the King of Ragtime.

HOT JAZZ ERA (1910–1944)

DIXIELAND

"**D**ixieland" is used as an umbrella term to cover the early musical styles of New Orleans and Chicago in the years prior to 1923, as well as jazz's development and revival in the 1930s. There are debates as to the exact definition of Dixieland. For some, it is exemplified by small bands of whatever colour playing improvised music. For others, the term is reserved for "white" musicians playing traditional jazz within the revivalist movement.

HOT

Above: A small New Orleans band playing improvised music.

NEW ORLEANS DIXIELAND (1900–1917)

New Orleans Dixieland, although not entirely limited to the location of New Orleans, had a particular sound associated with it. It has a very relaxed style, evoking the laid-back nature of the city. It had particular instrumentation and a rhythmic feeling because of the way the bands were organised. The "frontline" consisted of cornet, clarinet and trombone whilst the "backline" (rhythm section) contained tuba, banjo and drums. The origin of the deployment of instruments came from the marching bands with their backline accompanying the frontline and placing equal emphasis on all four beats of the measure. The bands would play as an ensemble – that is, playing together, with no solos.

Above: The Original Dixieland Jazz Band, formed in 1914.

The band that is credited with having released the first jazz recording is the Original Dixieland Jazz Band which put out "Livery Stable Blues" on the Victor & Columbia Records label in 1917. It was this record that made jazz available to a mass audience and it sold over a million copies.

The Original Dixieland Jazz Band

The Original Dixieland Jazz Band formed in 1914 under the leadership of cornet player Dominic "Nick" LaRocca. All members had played in Papa Jack Laine's Reliance Brass Band beforehand. They moved to Chicago in 1916 where they had limited success. It was in 1917, when they moved to New York, that they managed to obtain a top spot at a fashionable café, through the recommendation of Al Jolson who was soon to become famous in *The Jazz Singer*, the first "talkie". Their anarchic antics made them an instant hit and before long they recorded "Livery Stable Blues" which was listened to everywhere.

In April 1919 they went to play in London where they also recorded and had a big hit with the song "Soudan". They were invited to play at Buckingham Palace and were applauded by King George V for their famous tune "Tiger Rag". They also played at the Peace Ball at the Savoy Hotel in celebration of the end of the Great War. After they returned to America in the summer of 1920, their popularity began to wane. They split up in 1925 after LaRocca suffered a breakdown.

The Jazz Singer starring Al Jolson was released in 1927. It is widely credited as the first talking picture. In it Jolson plays the character Jakie Rabinowitz who, from an early age, is fascinated by jazz music, much to the chagrin of his orthodox Jewish family. Eventually he leaves home without their approval and begins a career as a jazz singer under the name of Jack Robin. At first he struggles as he works his way up through the nightclubs but eventually he achieves fame and fortune. He eventually returns home when he earns his

Above: Probably the first to record, rather than create, jazz – the Original Dixieland Jazz Band.

way into Broadway but he is still met with disapproval by his father who banishes him from the family home.

It is his opening night on Broadway, but Jolson's character is faced with the dilemma of whether to stand in for his sick father on the eve of Yom Kippur, the most sacred day of the Jewish faith, or to stand by the show business motto "the show must go on". At the rehearsal his mother informs him that his father is dying and initially pleads with him to return home. He is still determined to do the show, but eventually succumbs to the needs of his family. He returns, even though the producer of the show threatens that he will never work Broadway again. However, despite the fact that he sings at

the synagogue during the night of his father's passing, the producer believes in Jack Robin so much that he postpones the opening until the following night. There Jack triumphs over the audience and sings a song to his mother "Mammy".

Many more films followed which featured the sounds and heroes of jazz.

Whilst the Original Dixieland Jazz Band were the first "white" band to record, it was not until 1922 that the first "black" New Orleans band made a record. This was Kid Ory's Sunshine Orchestra who were based in California.

Above: Al Jolson – in The Jazz Singer.

BIOGRAPHY:

Kid Ory

Trombone

Edward "Kid" Ory was born in Louisiana in 1886. Originally he learned the banjo and fronted bands in his birth town of La Place. In 1913 he moved to New Orleans and changed to playing trombone. Here he led his own band called Kid Ory's Original Creole Jazz Band which saw an incredible line-up pass through its ranks, including many players who would go on to define hot jazz itself – Louis Armstrong, Joe Oliver, Mutt Carey, Johnny Dodds, Sidney Bechet, and Jimmie Noone amongst them.

In 1919 Ory moved to California and it was there in 1922 that his Sunshine Orchestra became the first New Orleans "black" band to make a record "Ory's Creole trombone" with "Society Blues". He stayed on the west coast for a number of years and then moved north to Chicago where he again featured top-class line-ups within his band. Whilst there he was reunited with Louis Armstrong and played on the "Hot Five" and "Hot Seven" recording sessions. He also performed alongside King Oliver and Jelly Roll Morton.

After a lull in his playing during the Depression years, Ory's career had a revival in the 1940s, which led to him appearing in films. He continued to tour and record until he retired in 1966.

Ory died in 1973.

Above: Kid Ory – leader of the first black band to cut a record.

CHICAGO DIXIELAND
(THE ROARING TWENTIES)

In the early 1920s Prohibition forced clubs and saloons across America to be closed down. The Storyville area of New Orleans that had once been a prosperous place for musicians soon fell into decline. Many of these musicians migrated north to Chicago, the "Windy" City, where illicit clubs called "speakeasies" remained open because they were run by gangsters and bootleggers. It was here that the New Orleans Dixieland sound combined with ragtime. Chicago, with its New Orleans influence, then became a breeding ground for many of the most innovative and important jazz players of the time.

During this period there were a great many social changes. Many people became rich in the stock market boom, women's hemlines became shorter as the "flapper" style became popular and life seemed to be the one big party portrayed in the escapist silent films of the day.

Chicago Dixieland differed by being played in 2/4 time – that is, the emphasis was placed on beats two and four of the measure. This reflected the aggressive hustle and bustle of the city. The instruments were augmented by adding saxophone and piano to the frontline and backline respectively and guitar and string bass replaced the banjo and tuba. The Chicago variant also featured instrumental solos, a concept introduced by Bix Beiderbecke, perfected by Joe "King" Oliver and revolutionised by Louis Armstrong.

Above: Kid Ory's Original Creole Jazz Band.

BIOGRAPHY:

Bix Beiderbecke

Cornet

Leon "Bix" Beiderbecke was born in March 1903 in Iowa. He came from a family of musicians and received formal musical training on the piano as a child. Although never fully proficient at sight reading, he nevertheless had a good ear for music and was able to repeat note for note whatever he heard. Ironically, he never received formal instruction in the instrument he became famous for, the cornet.

In 1921, he played with the Cy-Bix Orchestra, whilst studying at the Lake Forest Academy. However, his academic career was swiftly halted when he was expelled because of his alcoholism, a problem which would repeatedly dog his life.

He went to Chicago in 1923 and began working as a professional musician. Between then and 1928 he played with the likes of the Wolverines, Jean Goldkette and Frankie Trumbauer, all the while gaining a reputation for his astounding solos. He made a number of recordings, but it is the ones with Trumbauer, between February and May 1927, that are viewed as the peak of his recording career.

He joined the Paul Whiteman Orchestra, but in January 1929 was forced to leave due to alcohol-related problems. He came back temporarily amidst a number of health setbacks. By 1930 he was playing with the Jimmy Hicks Orchestra in Iowa and then went to Chicago in February to play with the Wingy Manone Band and Ted Weems. In April 1930 he arrived in New York City and played some one-night shows before he was due to rejoin Whiteman. However, he passed out and returned to Iowa to recuperate. Back in New York again, he played for only four days with the Casa Loma Orchestra before depression combined with his alcoholism caused him to give up altogether. He spent the rest of his time drifting aimlessly around

Above: Bix Beiderbecke.

New York City, although he did manage to write a few more compositions.

On 7 August 1931, Bix Beiderbecke died at the age of 29 due to complications related to his alcoholism.

Although Beiderbecke only had a career spanning ten years he had a profound influence on jazz history. The musician he most influenced to continue in this vein was probably an energetic black musician who went by the name of Louis Armstrong, who in turn was mentored by Joe "King" Oliver.

Above: Although Beiderbecke (second from the right) worked with many bands, he gained a reputation for his astounding solos.

BIOGRAPHY:

King Oliver

Cornet

Joe "King" Oliver was born in New Orleans in 1885. As a child he had been blinded and it was this that gave him his playing stance of leaning up against a wall, with a derby hat tilted over the bad eye. He originally learned to play trombone but soon took up the cornet whose sound he enhanced by using mutes such as bottles, cups and hats. At first he worked in the marching bands around New Orleans but was soon working with Kid Ory's band where he earned the nickname "King". When Ory moved to Chicago in 1917, Oliver went with

Above: King Oliver's Creole Jazz Band, "the first Afro-American jazz group to make a series of recordings".

him. He worked with Bill Johnson's Original Creole Orchestra and then the band of Lawrence Duke, from whom he took over in 1919, changing the band's name to King Oliver's Creole Jazz Band. It was this band that Louis Armstrong was to join as second cornettist and it also featured an amazing line-up of outstanding musicians including Johnny Dodds (clarinet), Baby Dodds (drums) and Louis Armstrong's wife Lil Hardin (piano).

It was in 1923 that the band made history by being "the first Afro-American jazz group to make a series of recordings". Songs that were recorded included "Chattanooga Stomp" and "High Society Rag" as well as Oliver's own "Riverside Blues", "Snag It" and "Working Man's Blues". In 1924 the band split up and Oliver went on to record with Jelly Roll Morton and took on a new band, the Dixie Syncopators. This band moved to New York in 1927 and in the 1930s, when Oliver was not working with them, he was a freelancer for the likes of Clarence Williams and vocalists such as Katherine Henderson and Eva Taylor.

Owing to Oliver's strange liking for sugar sandwiches his dental health began to deteriorate. He made his last recordings in 1931. Towards the end of the 1930s his playing suffered as he had lost most of his teeth. Sadly he was forced to give up his beloved music and he died in 1938, whilst working as a caretaker.

KING

BIOGRAPHY:

Louis Armstrong

Cornet/Trumpet

Daniel Louis Armstrong was born in August 1901 in New Orleans. After a childhood which involved both his parents deserting him and leaving him alone in the "red light" area of the city, he was forced into singing in the streets for small change.

He was arrested at the age of 13 and was sent to the Colored Waif's Home for Boys. There, he was able to study the cornet and played in the Waif's Home Band. He also earned his nickname "Satchmo" (derived from Satchelmouth). After leaving the orphanage, Armstrong worked at a number of jobs, all the time absorbing the music of local bands. His favourite artist was Joe "King" Oliver, who presented him with his own cornet and mentored him with further musical instruction. Satchmo went on to play with most of the best New Orleans "black" bands and also composed the jazz standard "I Wish I Could Shimmy Like My Sister Kate".

In 1919 he left New Orleans for St Louis and played on the river boats between the cities. Bands he played with included that of Kid Ory.

In 1922 Armstrong was invited by King Oliver and his Creole Jazz Band to join them in Chicago. In 1923 they made their first recording together and this relationship lasted for a year. After this, Satchmo, pushed on by his wife, Lil Hardin, whom he married in 1924, made a number

of recordings including those with the Fletcher Henderson Orchestra, the Clarence Williams Band and the blues singer Bessie Smith with whom he made "St Louis Blues".

It was in the period 1925 through to 1928, though, that Armstrong made the definitive recordings of his career and the first under his own name. These were with his "Hot Five" and "Hot Seven" groups and in this period he effectively reinvented jazz by establishing the soon-to-be standard 4/4 "swing" tempo and the theme-solo-theme structure. The influence of Beiderbecke showed as Louis placed the soloist at the centre of the music, with fully improvised chord-based solos consisting of a chorus length or more. All future jazz soloists would use the language that Armstrong laid out in describing a progression from the melody, to routineing the melody, to routineing the routine.

Above: Louis Armstrong — the first true virtuoso soloist of jazz.

From the late 20s to the 50s, Armstrong fronted large bands, usually of more than 15 musicians, often borrowing the personnel from other people's orchestras. His warm-hearted and larger-than-life personality meant other musicians were willing to record and play with him. He extensively toured all the major continents with his band the Louis Armstrong Allstars who were extremely popular everywhere they went and, as we shall see, also visited Britain. In the 1960s he scored a number of hit records including "Hello Dolly", knocking the Beatles off the number one spot, and "What A Wonderful World" in 1968. He continued to record and play until his death in July 1971.

The man who was responsible for many of the famous recordings from the hot jazz era was Clarence Williams, a musician of limited talent but an extraordinary businessman and visionary who brought the music to New York.

Above: "Satchmo" in his prime.

BIOGRAPHY:

Clarence Williams

Piano/Vocals

Clarence Williams was born in October 1893 in Louisiana. After a childhood spent entertaining patrons in his father's hotel, he joined a minstrel show as a singer, soon becoming the master of ceremonies. In 1906 he moved to the Storyville area where he became a hustler as well as piano player, vocalist and dancer. He always used to ensure that he knew the latest trends and kept himself informed of the hit songs out of New York. In between managing artists, running a laundry service and playing honky-tonks he composed songs and published them with his business partner Armand Piron.

In 1920 Williams moved to Chicago and opened a music store, which eventually led to him owning three stores. The following year he married Eva Taylor, who was both one of the first female vocalists and one of the first Afro-American vocalists to be heard on American radio. In 1923 he sold up in Chicago and moved to New York where, once again, his entrepreneurial skills proved successful with his publishing house. He sold his compositions to artists, put together groups to play his hit songs and then sold the sheet music. He also managed the blues singer Bessie Smith, although only until she realised her contractual obligation was direct to Columbia Records, not to Williams who had misinformed her.

In the same year he also became the A&R director for Okeh Records which allowed him to discover and develop new artists. He had a real ear for talent and amongst the musicians whose careers he helped advance were Louis Armstrong, Sidney Bechet, King Oliver, Coleman Hawkins, Buster Bailey, Cecil Scott and Willie "The Lion" Smith. He pulled tricks to ensure that the recording sessions he organised were the best possible, often using two studios in the same day if he did not like the results of the first one. When swing took over, Williams' compositions were less in demand, although he continued to compose until 1956, when he was involved in an accident which left him blind. He died in New York in 1965.

BIOGRAPHY:
Sidney Bechet

Clarinet/Saxophone

Sidney Bechet was born in New Orleans in 1897. He was largely self-taught and so good at the clarinet that he was soon playing in top local bands such as the Silver Bell Band. In 1917 he left, as had so many others, for Chicago and within a few years was playing with Louis Mitchell's Jazz Kings who regularly toured Europe. Bechet played in Britain with them as well with the Southern Syncopated Orchestra. It was there he found himself a soprano saxophone and changed over to it as his main instrument. In 1923 he made his first recording with Clarence Williams, and went on to do a number of classic sessions with the Clarence Williams Blue Five that also featured Louis Armstrong, who had been a childhood acquaintance, and Coleman Hawkins.

From 1925 to 1931 he lived in and performed around Europe, even spending a year in a French prison as a result of getting into a fight. After this he was deported and, having already been banned from England, he spent time in Berlin until 1931, after which he returned to America with the Noble Sissle Orchestra. In the 40s he was an integral part of the New York scene, particularly the Dixieland revival.

In 1952 Bechet returned to France and had great success with his recordings. He died in his adopted city of Paris in 1959.

Above: Sidney Bechet – the wizard of jazz.

BIOGRAPHY:

Billie Holiday

Vocals

Eleanora Fagan who was to become Billie Holiday, was born in Baltimore in 1915. Both her parents were in their early teens when she was born and were unmarried, her father a musician being absent most of the time. The young Eleanora's home life was considerably unstable and it was not long before she was behaving as a juvenile delinquent and even worked as a prostitute when she was 12.

In the late 1920s she and her mother moved to New York because of the Depression, earning their living in whatever way they could, including prostitution. By this time her father, Clarence Holiday, was working as a professional jazz musician and he joined the Fletcher Henderson band in the early 1930s. Eleanora changed her name to Billie Holiday, after her favourite film star, Billie Dove, and after her father. Following a failed audition as a dancer she managed to get a job as a singer. Thankfully, it was not long before her powerful and earthy voice ranged its way through the clubs and speakeasies of New York. She soon built up a fan base and John Hammond fortunately discovered her singing in Harlem and began to organise her professional life. In 1933 he set up the recording sessions with Benny Goodman which were effectively the start of her career and by the age of 20 Billie was regarded one of the hottest jazz singers, earning her the nickname "Lady Day" from Lester Young.

Throughout the 1930s she worked with the best bands of the time including Artie Shaw, Duke Ellington and Count Basie. By changing the tempos and rhythms her emotive voice added a new dimension to jazz. However, by 1938 she stepped out as a solo artist. For most of 1939 she was the resident artist at the Greenwich Village club "Café Society". It was here that she was first to express her condemnation of racism in the song "Strange Fruit", something that she had personally experienced, especially whilst on tour in the South the year before. Racism was something that she would battle against throughout her life.

In 1941 she married Jimmie Monroe. Although this was short-lived, by the end of the marriage she was totally addicted to opiates brought on by pain and depression. During the early 1940s she was earning over US$1000 a week; she was at the peak of her professional career with hits such as "God Bless The Child" but was spending most of her income in order to support her habit. In 1943 she was voted best jazz vocalist in Esquire magazines reader's poll. Because of this growing popularity Decca began making a series of thirty six recordings now regarded as among the greatest jazz recordings of all time.

In 1945, after marrying trumpet player Joe Guy she formed her own band, but owing to her drug problems this soon ended and in 1947 she was arrested. Billie spent a year and a day in a drug rehabilitation centre. Ten days after her release she played to a packed house at Carnegie Hall but was banned from playing in clubs.

Sadly, from 1950 onward her life was plagued by her heroin and alcohol addiction.

In 1954 Billie toured Europe, including a concert at London's Albert Hall before an audience of 6000. In 1956 her autobiography "The Lady sings the Blues" was released which exposed her sordid life to her fans.

Unfortunately her talent had now faded and the rest of her life was a downhill struggle against her addictions. Her life dramatically ended on 15th July 1959 whilst she was under arrest for possession of heroin whilst in a New York hospital.

Above: Billie Holiday - The Lady sings the Blues.

BOOGIE WOOGIE

Boogie woogie originated in noise-filled bars and developed its rich, full-bodied sound because of the need to compensate for there being only a single piano player instead of a full-blown orchestra or band. It is played on the blues chord progression with a repeated rolling bass line via the left hand and a synchronous eight-note melody via the right hand. The eight beats to the measure give boogie woogie its signature feel.

In the 1930s boogie woogie was utilised in many jazz recordings, particularly as the tempos speeded up. Indeed a craze followed and in the 1940s many of the big bands started to include boogie woogie arrangements in their repertoires. Its addition helped bring jazz to a wider audience and led to a major developmental movement in jazz piano playing, led by Earl "Fatha" Hines. Boogie woogie also had a great influence on the development of early rock 'n' roll music in the 1950s.

Above: Led by Earl "Fatha" Hines, boogie woogie had a great influence on the early rock 'n' roll music of the 1950s.

BIOGRAPHY:

Earl Hines

Piano

Earl Kenneth Hines was born in Pennsylvania in 1905. He moved to Chicago in 1923 and this is when his career as a professional musician began to bloom. He played with several orchestras as well as recording a number of piano solos including his famous "57 Varieties" which was to become a standard for future jazz pianists. It was his imaginative style and technique in using both hands to produce unusual rhythmic effects and accents that allowed him to become a jazz pioneer. The recordings which most exemplify his career are the 1928 "Hot Five" and "Hot Seven"sides with Louis Armstrong. The pairing seemed to spark the best in both musicians as can be heard on the song "Fireworks" and on Hines' own composition "A Monday Date".

In 1928 he also made his debut as a bandleader in his own right, and continued as a leader until 1948, after which he again played with Louis Armstrong, this time with the Allstars. In the 1950s he formed a Dixieland band due to a revived interest in that style but which never achieved the critical acclaim of his earlier work. All that was to change, though, in 1964 when he recorded his album *Earl Hines Live At the Village Vanguard* which is still seen as one of the top jazz records of all time. His career flourished until he died in California in 1983, just two days after performing to a sold-out audience.

Above: Earl Hines — the first modern jazz pianist.

SWING

The golden age of swing was from the early 1930s through to the late 1940s, usually referred to as the big band era. Whereas prior to this musicians had played in only small groups of less than ten or even solo, Swing emphasised the sound of the big band, all designed to encourage people to dance. The instrumentalists were grouped within the band, each playing their own short melodies in call-and-response patterns. It was essential that everyone played in tune and kept a protocol on how they kept the rhythm, whether it was on the beat, or behind or on top of it. Usually the emphasis was on four beats to the bar and swing became extremely popular because of the buoyant rhythms inherent in it. Although the bands had mainly a collective sound most bands concentrated on arrangements that allowed them to play for great lengths of time. However, there was still space for soloists to perform in a lyrical way within the framework of the composition.

Songs that were played with hard-driven rhythms and extensive improvisations were known as "hot", whereas those played in a softer way were referred to as "sweet". Indeed, many of the bands from that time were tagged as either one or the other, even though their repertoires usually covered all the different sounds.

Owing to the musicians having to ensure that they co-ordinated their playing together, swing musicians were usually put through rigorous rehearsals and the bandleaders ensured that they played well as a unit. One bandleader who strove for a controlled balance amongst his players was Count Basie.

Above: Glenn Miller and his orchestra gained popularity through their broadcasts on NBC radio in the 1930s.

BIOGRAPHY:

Count Basie

Piano

William "Count" Basie was born in New Jersey in 1904. During his childhood he was trained in music and the piano by his mother. In the 1920s he moved to New York and it was there that he met many of the Harlem piano greats such as Thomas "Fats" Waller, who mentored Basie, and Willie Smith. Basie spent his time learning his trade in the saloons and cabarets of Harlem and touring the vaudeville theatres.

In 1929 Basie went on the road with the Bennie Moten band in Kansas City and this lasted until 1935, when Moten died. Basie took over as bandleader and the band was renamed the Count Basie Orchestra. Following the Kansas City tradition, the band was content to play for hours on end using extended variations that eventually transformed themselves into songs.

They took their act to New York but at first were deemed to be too loud and rough. However, by the end of the 1930s they had acquired an almost fanatical following and both the collective sound of the band and the individual players were to influence jazz in a huge way, particularly Joe Jones in Basie's "All-American Rhythm Section" and Lester Young, one of his tenor saxophonists (see bebop). The band excelled at a riffing style which can be heard in their famous "One O'Clock Jump". This thematic riff was to form the basis of swing. Throughout the 1940s they continued to tour and also had international hit records.

By 1950 Basie's original band had split up but within two years he was to put together a new band, although he relied on outside arrangers to give them their slick sound this time. This band was to become a jazz institution and was the training ground for many young musicians on their tours.

In 1976 Basie suffered a heart attack but continued to work from a wheelchair. He died in California in 1984, having succumbed to cancer.

One of the biggest changes to take place in the transition from early jazz to swing was in the drums. The drummer who single-handedly redefined jazz drumming was "Papa" Joe Jones. Early drums used the bass drum on every beat and this is known as four-beats-to-the-bar. It was often necessary to have more than one drummer in a band to cover playing the snare and cymbals as well. Jones took this idea and threw it out of the window, instead utilising the ride cymbals as the main time-keeping device, and playing bass drum on the first and third instead of on every beat and the hi-hat cymbals on the second and fourth beats. His sound also gave the Basie band an instantly recognisable sound.

The man who earned the title "the King of Swing" was Benny Goodman and he is widely regarded as the man who made swing popular with the masses.

Above: William "Count" Basie.

BIOGRAPHY:

Benny Goodman

Clarinet

Benny Goodman was born in Chicago in 1909. As a child he received a formal training in music and the clarinet. After the death of his father, Goodman played the local dance halls. He then moved around the States, performing with bands such as the Ben Pollack Band. He picked up the Dixieland clarinet style through his introduction to the New Orleans Rhythm Kings and also picked up the alto sax.

He was an integral part of the early Chicago-wide group of musicians, nowadays collectively known as "The Chicagoans", that included Pee Wee Russell, Frankie Teschmacher, Leon Rapolo, Max Kaminsky, Jimmy McPartland and his brother Charles, Muggsy Spanier, the Dorsey brothers, Glenn Miller and many others. As such, Goodman is considered to be one of the "inventors" of the American swing band.

In 1922, he appeared onstage with the Benny Meroff Orchestra, in Chicago, doing an imitation of the clarinettist Ted Lewis, who was then America's favourite. Not long afterwards, Ben Pollack sent for him to join the Pollack Orchestra at the Venice ballroom in LA. Goodman's first recorded solo, "He's the Last Word", was with the Pollack Orchestra, in Chicago on 12 December 1926. He left Pollack in 1929 and became a successful "studio" musician in New York City. In the summer of 1932 Goodman formed his first band, starring singer Russ Columbo.

In the aftermath of the Great Depression of the late 20s and early 30s, a new generation of young people was looking for music that they could call their own. Goodman's orchestra was destined to fill this need. The hot bands of the 20s and early 1930s like Fletcher Henderson, Coon-Sanders' Nighthawks, and Don Redman had all been disbanded. The only real competition Goodman had was the Casa Loma Orchestra.

Above: Benny Goodman, one of "The Chicagoans".

In 1934 he formed his second band, which had more regular work, for a residency at Billy Rose's Music Hall. Along with making some interesting recordings, the band appeared on the three-hour Coast to Coast NBC radio programme called *Let's Dance*. Goodman's orchestra shared the *Let's Dance* show with the Kel Murray Orchestra, a straight-ahead dance band, and Xavier Cugat's Latin "Waldorf-Astoria Hotel" Orchestra, a society dance band.

NBC's *Let's Dance* show was actually a five-hour broadcast from New York staged so that all US time zones would get three hours of music. The east coast and central time zones were cut off after the first three hours; Mountain Time zone listened to hours two–four, while the West Coast listened to hours three–five. In this manner, all American listeners heard three solid hours of dance music over the airwaves. Six months later, MCA booked Benny's orchestra for a coast-to-coast tour which turned out to be almost totally unsuccessful and, on several occasions during the tour, MCA considered cancelling. That was, until the band reached its last date at the Palomar Ballroom in Los Angeles. There Goodman found his audience. The "kids" went completely wild over Goodman's swing sound.

When he brought back his orchestra to New York's Paramount Theatre, the kids were actually dancing in the aisles. "Bobbysox-ers" were invented and "jitterbugs" became endemic. Benny Goodman was crowned as the "King of Swing", a title he was to hold for the rest of his life. After his extended Palomar engagement, the band headed back east, stopping over in Chicago for still another extended run, this time at the Joseph Urban Room at the Congress Hotel.

In 1935, Benny Goodman And His Orchestra played the Congress Hotel in Chicago. The band included such outstanding musicians as Gene Krupa on drums; Jess Stacy, piano; Nate Kabier, trumpet; Hymie Shertzer, alto sax; Art Rollini, tenor sax; Allen Reuss, guitar; Harry Goodman (Benny's brother), bass; and Helen Ward, one of the best big band vocalists. Earlier, Goodman had made some trio recordings using Krupa and pianist Teddy Wilson that had sold well. Helen Oakley, later Helen Oakley Dance, encouraged him to feature Wilson, who was black, in the trio at the hotel. Thankfully, Goodman was persuaded that featuring a racially mixed group was not a recipe for disaster in those segregated times and the occasion passed without public comment. Wilson was soon to became a regular member of the Goodman trio. This was a historic moment in American music history. It was the first time that a "white" band had hired a black musician to play with it on stage and Goodman continued with this innovation until it became accepted.

In 1936, Benny added Lionel Hampton, the vibraphonist, to form the Benny Goodman Quartet. Though this was not the first integrated jazz group, it had by far the highest profile. Goodman's big band was continuing to attract huge and enthusiastic audiences, and was featuring such sidemen as Harry James, Ziggy Elman, Chris Griffin, Vernon Brown, Babe Russin and Art Rollini. Starting in March 1937, Goodman began an especially successful engagement at New York's Paramount theatre. His records were also selling well.

At the start, when Benny's orchestra was little-known, it was basically a dance band, occasionally playing some "hot" music. There was little income, and Benny was working hard to build his band's "book" of arrangements. Before the 1934–1935 period, throughout it and afterwards too, most of the Goodman orchestra's book had been written by Spud Murphy. The "killer-dillers" (like "Sing, Sing, Sing") in the Goodman book, were almost all written by Jimmy Mundy and Spud Murphy. Benny was also just beginning to pick up some scores from Fletcher Henderson.

In 1939, after Fletcher Henderson's Orchestra disbanded, Benny hired him. By this time, Goodman's orchestra was enormously successful. Fletcher then presented Benny with many of his own band's scores. Benny continued to use Fletcher and Horace Henderson, Edgar Sampson, Benny Carter and Deane Kincaide scores throughout his career with Mary Lou Williams contributing the famous "Roll 'Em". To Benny's credit, he never failed to acknowledge Fletcher Henderson's co-authorship of the big band swing sound even though Goodman, himself, had played a huge part in the invention of that sound.

After Henderson, Benny went on to hire musicians such as Cootie Williams (trumpet), Charlie Christian (guitar) and "Slam" Stewart (bass fiddle) as well as singers such as Ella Fitzgerald and Jimmy Rushing, again all black artists.

Benny should also be remembered for establishing the "personality" concept in big band swing. It was in Benny's band that the sidemen were given public exposure as soloists. This fan worship for Goodman sidemen such as Harry James, Gene Krupa, Lionel Hampton and Ziggy Elman later allowed them to go on and form their own orchestras. Among his female vocalists were Helen Ward, Peggy Lee and Louise Tobin. This practice of featuring the sidemen was picked up by virtually every other swing orchestra of the day although rarely does Benny receive sufficient credit for this.

In 1939, Benny switched recording companies from RCA to Columbia. He also signed Eddie Sauter as his new arranger. It was Sauter who rejected Goodman's original brasses-against-the-saxes format for a newer and more harmonically advanced type of scoring, especially for the ballads. Sauter was responsible for such hits as "Clarinet à la King" and "Benny Rides Again".

In 1941, Benny married Alice Duckworth, the sister of John Hammond, the famous jazz critic and another believer in racial equality. It was a very happy, long-lived marriage.

Another unique contribution of Goodman's was the concept of a band within a band, with the development of his magnificent Trios (1935), Quartet, and Sextet. These small group sessions with Lionel Hampton, Teddy Wilson and Gene Krupa are as live and vibrant today as when they were first recorded – surely the hallmark of genius. After the end of the big band era, Goodman went on to a career as a classical clarinet soloist with many of the world's great symphony orchestras.

Nobody, but absolutely nobody, played the clarinet as well as Benny. He drilled his band to perfection by demanding no less from the sidemen than he did of himself. He was not only well liked by the bandsmen, but also very much admired for his musicianship. He stands as a giant among jazz musicians.

He died in New York in June 1986.

Jazz started at a time of great racial tension where segregation was considered normal and non-white musicians had few rights. The white musicians who were pro-racial integration often ran into difficulties. Some find it strange that the band to have made the first jazz recording, the Original Dixieland Jazz Band, was white. However, a black bandleader had been approached but had turned down the opportunity in case his musical ideas were stolen.

Fortunately, in the century that has passed since jazz first began, many of the racial barriers in the world have been broken down. Some of the credit for this should be given to jazz with its democratic approach to sound.

Above: Benny Goodman – the King of Swing.

BIOGRAPHY:

The Dorsey Brothers

Jimmy: Cornet/Saxophone
Tommy: Trombone

Jimmy Dorsey was born in February 1904. His brother Tommy was born in November of the following year. They lived in an area of Shenandoah, Pennsylvania where coal mining was the main industry and although their father had started off as a coal miner he was able to teach both his sons music as he was not only the leader of the Elmore Band but a music teacher.

Jimmy studied the slide trumpet and cornet and from the early age of seven was playing cornet in his father's band. In September 1913, he appeared briefly (for two days) in a New York theatre variety act with J. Carson McGee's King Trumpeters. In 1915 he made the switch to the saxophone. Tommy in the meantime learned to play both the trumpet and the trombone, which was the instrument he was to become famous for. He also became famous for his temperamental nature which would lead to both tension and creativity between the two brothers.

Around 1917, the brothers formed a group called Dorsey's Novelty Six that later became Dorsey's Wild Canaries. The group found work in Baltimore where they also became one of the first jazz groups to broadcast. Following their Baltimore residency, they disbanded and the Dorseys joined Billy Lustig's Scranton Sirens. It was here that they made their first recordings of "Three O'Clock In The Morning" and "Fate".

Throughout the 1920s, Jimmy Dorsey played in a variety of orchestras including those of Paul Whiteman and Vincent Lopez. By September 1924, he was playing with the California Ramblers, and from 1925 on, did much freelance radio and recording. In 1930 Jimmy joined the Ted Lewis Orchestra with which he took part in a tour of Europe. He left Lewis in August 1930, returned to the USA, and found work with the Andre Kostelanetz, Jacques Renard, Rudy Vallee, Victor Young and Rubinoff orchestras amongst others. Tommy, in the meantime, lent his "hot" style to many of the smaller bands around and cut a number of hot recordings in the late 1920s including his own composition "Three Moods". He also appeared in a couple of films.

Although the brothers had had their own orchestra cutting records before 1934 it was not until the spring of that year that the Dorseys were to form their own full-time band. At first they toured outside of New York City, but in July 1934 they made their official debut at the Sands Point Beach Club, in Long Island City, New York, the first of many dates. This band featured both Glenn Miller and Bob Crosby, the brother of Bing Crosby. However, it was not to last long. Sibling rivalry had always been a problem, and it came to a head in May 1935. The Dorsey Brothers' Orchestra was playing at a famous New York casino. Tommy had decided on a tune and was

Above: Jimmy Dorsey.

just giving the band the tempo when Jimmy made a derogatory comment about it. It is said that Tommy just picked up his trombone, played a raspberry and stormed off. After this Jimmy took on the responsibility of leader, and the band became the Jimmy Dorsey Orchestra with all the personnel remaining loyal to Jimmy.

The 1938 Jimmy Dorsey Orchestra, with Bob Eberle (brother of the bandleader Ray Eberle) on vocals, consisted of Jimmy, Milt Yaner, Herbie Hamyer, Leonard Whitney and Charles Frazier on saxophones; Ralph Muzzillo, Shorty Sherock and Don Mattison on trumpets; Bobby Byrne and Sonny Lee on trombones; Ray McKinley on drums; Roc Hilman on guitar; Jack Ryan on bass and Freddy Slack on piano. In 1939 they were joined by a second vocalist, Helen O'Connell. It was in 1940 that the orchestra achieved one of their biggest-selling hits with their recording of "The Breeze and I" followed by the 1941 hit "Maria Elena", both featuring just Eberle. That same year both vocalists were heard in more of the band's biggest hit recordings, like "Amapola" and "Green Eyes". In 1942, Eberle and O'Connell teamed up on the Jimmy Dorsey hit recording of "Tangerine". The 1943 recording of "Besame Mucho" (Kiss Me Much) with Bob Eberle was another hit record although later that year O'Connell was to leave the orchestra.

Jimmy made a number of film appearances such as *Ship Ahoy*, *That Girl From Paris*, *Shall We Dance*, *I Dood It* (directed by Vincente Minnelli), *Lost In A Harem*, *4 Jacks and a Jeep* and the 1947 biopic *The Fabulous Dorseys* which was to eventually reunite the brothers.

Having left the Dorsey Orchestra, Tommy formed his own orchestra from the remnants of the Joe Haymes band that was then playing at the Hotel McAlpin in New York. Their first recordings were made in September 1935. A few months later, while playing the Blue Room of the Hotel Lincoln, he instituted several personnel changes by looting other people's bands. These included Dave Tough on drums, Bud Freeman on tenor sax and the Three Esquires, consisting of Joe Bauer on trumpet, Jack Leonard on vocals and Odd Stordahl, an arranger who was later to become known as Axel Stordahl and who did many of the arrangements for Frank Sinatra. Together they made recordings such as "Sweetheart of Sigma Chi" and "Once in a While".

As well as his own orchestra Tommy would also form smaller groups from his own band members as well as freelance with the likes of Louis Armstrong and Jack Teagarden. In the 1940s, he turned his attention to the "hot" sounds of arranger Sy Oliver of the Jimmy Lunceford Orchestra as well as formulating his own trademark moody numbers. He added renowned drummer Buddy Rich (a relationship which was to continue after Rich had returned from the war) and Frank Sinatra. Although the three were all renowned for their temperaments it was this that kept the group dynamically "hot and cool" between upbeat drum rhythms and ballads.

During the war Tommy lost some of his key personnel to the draft which caused him to add a string section in order to amplify the band's sound. After the war he ditched it and returned to an even bigger horn section and thus even more of a big-band sound.

Although for many years following the casino incident the brothers refused to speak to each other, it was the film *The Fabulous Dorseys* released in 1947, that was finally to reunite them – although this still took until the spring of 1953. It was then that Jimmy rejoined Tommy and together they were billed as The Fabulous Dorseys' Orchestra, even hosting their own show on American television. Sadly, Tommy died in 1956 at which point Jimmy took over the role as leader again although because of cancer he soon had to hand over to Lee Castle. In 1957 Jimmy Dorsey died. However, the orchestra was to continue for many years under the guidance of Castle.

Many of the songs deemed as swing classics were composed by Duke Ellington, a man who remained in the artistic vanguard of jazz throughout his career.

Above: Tommy Dorsey.

BIOGRAPHY:

Duke Ellington

Piano

Edward Kennedy Ellington was born in Washington DC in 1899. He earned the nickname "Duke" because of his witty humour and stylish dress sense. He was an accomplished pianist, particularly in the stride style. At the age of 18 he formed his first small band in his hometown. In 1923, Ellington moved to New York City and started to play with the Elmer Snowden Orchestra at the Hollywood Inn, just off Broadway. Snowden had been cheating the band of money and when his personnel discovered this they threw him out and made Ellington their new leader. In 1925, after a deliberate fire set by the club's owners, due to an insurance scam, the Ellington band was renamed the "Washingtonians" when the Hollywood re-opened as the Washington Club. Their theme song at the time was "East St Louis Toodle Oo" which highlighted the band's "jungle sound" of their "plunge-mute" trumpeter Bubber Miley. After a further change to the club's name the band was known as Duke Ellington and his Kentucky Club Orchestra, although most of their recordings were still made as the Washingtonians until 1929.

By 1927, Ellington signed a contract with band agent Irving Mills that gave Mills 50 per cent of Ellington's earnings and 55 per cent of any song royalties on Ellington's compositions. In return Mills arranged for Ellington to be booked in as the house band at the Cotton Club, after the residency had been refused by King Oliver. Owing to the band's renown for their jungle-style music, some of their recordings at this time were credited to Duke Ellington and the Jungle Band.

His singers were Ivie Anderson, Ray Nance, Kay Davis and Adelaide Hall, who was one of the chorus girls at the club,. One day while the Duke was rehearsing the band for "Creole Love Call", he overheard Adelaide humming along. She was asked to sing in front of the band and appeared on the recording. which was to become one of Ellington's biggest hits.

The Duke, as well as being a proficient bandleader, was highly skilled in arranging and writing around his band's respective skills and it was through this that many jazz legends were able to hone their musical talents. As well as the aforementioned Bubber Miley, who was sadly fired in 1929 because of alcoholism, many other musicians were to work in the ranks of the Duke's band including his permanent baritone saxophonist Harry Carney, alto Johnny Hodges, trombonists "Tricky" Sam Nanton and Juan Tizol and clarinettist Barney Bigard; the latter two would compose some of Ellington's biggest hits. The Duke's fairness and progressive vision meant that many band members stayed with the band for over 50 years. In 1931 the Ellington band left their residency at the Cotton Club and went on tour as Duke Ellington and his Orchestra in the USA and Europe.

With the advent of better recording technology it was Ellington who recorded some of the longest 78s of the time including "Tiger Rag" in 1929, the first double-sided jazz record, and "Creole Rhapsody" in 1931.

In 1932 he co-wrote the song that was to define the swing era with "It Don't Mean a Thing (If It Ain't Got That Swing)" which was to allow the band to make the transition from hot jazz to swing. In 1933 the band went to Europe and were met in England with an extraordinary reception.

In the decades that followed, the Ellington Orchestra continued to produce jazz standards such as "Satin Doll" and Ellington was to work in star line-ups alongside jazz greats Louis Armstrong and John Coltrane.

Ellington died in 1974 after a battle with cancer at which point his son took over the band.

One of the best-known swing bands of all time, and one which evokes memories of World War II, is the Glenn Miller Band.

Above: Duke Ellington – the elegant bandleader.

BIOGRAPHY:

Glenn Miller

Trombone/Bandleader

Glenn Miller was born in March 1904 in Clarinda, Iowa. His first instrument was a mandolin, given to him by his father, but he soon exchanged it for a horn. Although he attended university, his musical interests meant he dropped out to concentrate on his career. He worked at a number of jobs including as a sideman in touring bands and after heading to Los Angeles played in the Ben Pollack orchestra alongside Benny Goodman. He also worked freelance in New York in theatre pit bands and on radio broadcasts as well as starting his career as an arranger and composer. His original tunes included his theme song "Moonlight Serenade".

In the early 1930s Miller was to play with the original Dorsey Brothers' Orchestra and in 1934 became their musical director. He also directed the bands led by John Scott Trotter and the actor and singer Smith Ballew in 1932.

In 1937 he formed his own orchestra which was to be short-lived as they had not yet discovered their definitive sound. By January 1938, after playing in hotels, a few radio broadcasts, making some recordings for Brunswick and Decca, and playing a hotel as house band in Bridgeport, Connecticut, Miller decided to disband and return to New York. Strangely, he never felt confident in his trombone-playing skills, having worked alongside some of the top hot players of the time, such as Jack Teagarden and because of this he often ducked out of solo spots when he had his own band.

By early spring of 1938, Miller had decided to form a new orchestra but this time he adjusted the line-up and the arrangements so that the reed section led the orchestra. The clarinet would lead and the saxophones, particularly the tenor sax, would play the same melody but one octave lower than the clarinet. He retained many of the musicians from his first band including his close friend Chummy MacGregor on piano and Hal MacIntyre on alto. New additions included Tex Beneke on tenor sax, Willie Schwartz arrived to play the leading clarinet and Ray Eberle, the younger brother of the Dorsey Brothers' singer Bob, was the male vocalist. Their female vocalist at the time was Gail Reece.

This second band was to prove most successful. In June 1938, they were performing at the Paradise Restaurant in New York City. The band received national radio broadcasts through NBC, gaining further popularity. They also added Marion Hutton, the sister of Hollywood actress Betty Hutton, to their line-up as female vocalist later that year. By 1939, the band was recording for the RCA Victor Bluebird label with hits such as "Tuxedo Junction", "In the Mood" and "Pennsylvania 6-5000". They were also booked in up and down the east coast of America including a long stint at the Meadowbrook Ballroom in Cedar Grove, New Jersey, which also included broadcasts.

In October, the Miller band, along with the bands of Paul Whiteman and Benny Goodman's, played at

Carnegie Hall where they soon got the audience up and dancing. In December 1939 they started their three-times-a-week CBS radio broadcasts, promoting Chesterfield cigarettes. In January 1940 they also started a long stay at the Cafe Rouge of the Hotel Pennsylvania in New York City. The Modernaires vocal group came on board in early 1941. In March, the orchestra starred in and played the soundtrack for the 20th Century Fox film *Sun Valley Serenade*, which featured skater Sonja Henie and John Payne. A year later, they were back in Hollywood for their second film, *Orchestra Wives*.

Above: Glenn Miller – the Moonlight Serenader.

"Chattanooga Choo Choo", a song featured in their first film, became the first million-selling record. To commemorate this, RCA Victor presented Miller with a gold-plated record which is the way that million-sellers have been marked ever since. When World War II broke out, Miller gave a series of Saturday afternoon performances at various military camps across the USA. These were broadcast as the *Sunset Serenade* shows, the first of which was aired on 30 August 1941.

The last engagement of Miller's civilian orchestra was on 26 September 1942 at the Central Theatre in Passaic, New Jersey. They performed their most popular songs, including "In the Mood", "Moonlight Cocktail" and "I've Got a Gal in Kalamazoo". Overcome by emotion, they were barely able to play their "Moonlight Serenade" theme for the last time together. By then, the band was at the peak of success and popularity, and Miller was receiving a huge income from recordings, broadcasts, product endorsements and personal appearances. However, he felt a need to do more for the United States' war effort. In October 1942 he was assigned to the Specialist Corps of the US Army. He persuaded the army commanders to "modernise" the army band and thus raise troop morale by arranging concerts. Having agreed with his suggestions, his superiors appointed him captain and he was transferred to the Army Air Corps where he formed the Glenn Miller Army Air Force Band.

In 1943 he and his band were sent to England to raise morale over there. In December 1944 Major Glenn Miller boarded a plane for Paris and was never seen again. To this day the exact cause of his death remains a mystery. Tex Beneke took over the band and they stayed together for many years, touring and recording, all the while retaining the Glenn Miller name.

Above: Major Glenn Miller and his band during the early 1940s.

BIOGRAPHY:

Paul Whiteman

Bandleader/Viola

Paul Whiteman was born in 1887. His father, Wilberforce, was the Superintendent for Musical Education in the Denver, Colorado public school system. As such, he was responsible for developing the musical talents of a great many other youngsters, including Jimmie Lunceford. In 1915 Whiteman, a then-viola player out of the San Francisco Symphony Orchestra, was captivated by the sound of jazz and filled with ambition to play it. He joined the John Tait Band, only to be fired after just one day when it was discovered that he could not play jazz. But he was to meet Ferde Grofe, Tait's pianist, on that eventful day.

In 1917 the US Army turned Whiteman down because of his obesity, but the US Navy picked him up as a bandleader. In 1918 he formed his first civilian band, the Paul Whiteman Orchestra, for the Fairmont Hotel in San Francisco, and also played dates in and around LA before settling in the Hotel Alexandria in LA at the end of 1919. His pianist was Ferde Grofe, who was Whiteman's own age, and who had also been a viola player with the LA Symphony Orchestra before concentrating on the piano. After three years as pianist with Paul, he became the band's full-time arranger/composer. Other pianists who followed Grofe were Roy Bargy, Lennie Hayton and Ray Turner.

In 1920, Whiteman's band began their Victor recordings, and he achieved national fame. In 1923, a musical instrument company named him "King of Jazz" as part of a promotional event, and this title would remain with Whiteman forever, rightly or wrongly. His was the most popular "white" band of the 1920s.

Above: Paul Whiteman – the King of Jazz, according to some.

Jack Teagarden

Trombone/Vocals

Whiteman's orchestra was the first in many areas. It was the first to popularise arrangements and use full reed and brass sections. It was the first big band to play in vaudeville, travel to Europe, use a female singer (Mildred Bailey, who was Al Rinker's sister) and the first to feature a vocal trio, known as the Rhythm Boys, consisting of Al Rinker, Harry Barris and Bing Crosby, who all got their breaks in this band. Virtually every musician or soloist of note played in the Whiteman orchestra at one time or another, including Jack Teagarden. In 1924, Whiteman introduced George Gershwin's *Rhapsody in Blue*, which he had had specially commissioned, at the historic Aeolian Hall Concert in New York City. This became the orchestra's signature tune.

In 1930 Whiteman appeared in the appropriately-named film *The King of Jazz*. Unfortunately, in the 1940s his orchestra, along with many other swing orchestras, began to lose popularity and so Whiteman started to work as a musical director for a television company. However, at times he did put a band together for special occasions. Whiteman died in 1967 after several years spent in retirement.

Jack Teagarden is widely regarded as one of the best trombonists in jazz history due to his skill in getting as wide a range and as much power as possible whilst moving the slide as little as possible.

Jack Teagarden was born in Texas in August 1905. His mother first taught him to read music and then the pair would play piano in the local cinemas to accompany the silent films of the time. When he was seven his father gave him a trombone and he learned to play it, eventually leading his own band in high school. He was also an astounding singer.

He moved to New York in 1927 and in 1928 made his first recording with Roger Kahn's band: "She's a Great Great Girl". Further recordings soon followed owing to the incredible talent he had shown and he found himself in great demand by other performers. He recorded alongside Benny Goodman, Red Nichols and Louis Armstrong, and in 1933 signed up with the Paul Whiteman Orchestra, for five years.

In 1939 Teagarden formed his own band that continued to play until 1946. After this he rejoined Louis Armstrong in his Allstars band. For the last part of his career he led a Dixieland sextet, playing with Earl Hines amongst others.

He died in New Orleans in 1964

Above: Jack Teagarden – "the best trombonist in history!"

BIOGRAPHY:

Ella Fitzgerald

Trombone/Vocals

Ella was born in Newport News, Virginia in 1917. Fifteen years later she was orphaned and sent first to an orphanage in Riverdale, and then to the New York state training school for girls. Sadly, systematic abuse was widespread and she ran away.

She began living on the streets of New York along with many other children from similar backgrounds. In 1934 when she was 16 she made her singing debut at the amateur night at the famous Apollo theatre in Harlem where she won first prize and was discovered by band leader Chick Webb.

After some coaching by Chick she began her career as the lead singer in his orchestra at the Savoy Ballroom. In 1938 she had her first hit record based on a nursery rhyme called "A Tisket, a Tasket", followed by "Undecided" a year later. When Chick died that same year Ella took over leadership of his band until 1942 when she launched her solo career after marrying Benjamin Korngay.

In 1946 she became the star attraction at the legendary "Jazz at the Philharmonic" shows organised by Norman Granz of Verve Records, who was also her manager and collaborator for over 40 years. Under his direction she recorded her renowned "songbook" albums - a series of albums each devoted to the songs of a particular American composer. Granz also produced her recordings with Duke Ellington and Count Basie. Having divorced Korngay she married bass player Ray Brown in 1948 but sadly this marriage also ended in divorce.

Between 1956 and 1964 Ella recorded songbook albums featuring the music of Cole Porter, Rodgers and Hart, Duke Ellington, Irving Berlin, George and Ira Gershwin, Harold Arlen, Jerome Kern and Johnny Mercer. These albums widened her fame making her one of the handful of jazz musicians who are household names, as well as helping to define what is referred to as the "Great American Songbook".

Although Ella sang solidly in a swing to be-bop style her music never seemed to go out of fashion. During the 1960s she filled US college auditoriums with rebellious students and also appealed to lounge lizards in the early 90s. Ella had a hugely successful career spanning six decades, yielding thousands of recordings and earning her countless awards including honorary doctorate degrees and 13 Grammy awards.

Despite never having received any formal musical training her technique and range rivalled that of operatic divas and her improvisational talents were on a par with the greatest jazz instrumentalists. Ella was also a diabetic for many years and although the disease affected her vision and resulted in the amputation of both her legs she continued to perform until 1992 when, sadly, she became too frail to continue.

Ella Fitzgerald died on June 15 1996.

Above: Ella Fitzgerald - the First Lady of Song

PROGRESSIVE SWING

When the big-band era declined after the war years of the late 40s, a new style emerged. Progressive swing, which was also known as progressive jazz, had a darker, more dissonant sound than earlier swing. This style, which borrowed techniques from European composers like Stravinsky and Shostakovich, is most associated with Stan Kenton who is regarded as the influential figure in this part of jazz history.

BIOGRAPHY:

Stan Kenton

Piano

Stan Kenton was born in Kansas in 1911. He first studied composition and piano with his mother, and then with a theatre organist. He then went on to study with Earl Hines (strangely enough without using an actual piano as they both had enough perfect pitch to learn on a wooden board with the keys drawn on). After Kenton finished school he toured with several small bands and in 1933 he landed a job with Everett Hoagland's band, which had a booking at the Rendezvous Ballroom in California. He played in a number of house bands but it was not until May 1941 that he put together his own band in order to realise his own musical aspirations. He also wrote the arrangements and compositions, including the song which gave his first orchestra its name: "Artistry in Rhythm".

Above: Stan Kenton – a progressive man.

BIOGRAPHY:

Woody Herman

Clarinet/Saxophone

Kenton challenged his musicians in his quest for the right sound in his band. In 1947 his band was called the Progressive Jazz Orchestra and included a brass section featuring five trombones and five trumpets. As the years passed, numbers grew bigger and by 1950 he had a touring 40-piece band, even adding a string section. He was also one of the first to incorporate a Cuban sound in his music by adding conga and bongo drums.

Later on, in the 50s and 60s, Kenton was to add French horns and mellophoniums. During this time he was still touring and even going to American college campuses in order to encourage other young musicians. His experimentations continued throughout his career and in 1965 he played concert music with his Los Angeles Neophonic Orchestra.

Throughout Kenton's career he always pushed the boundaries of jazz. He died in August 1979.

Woody Herman was one of the most popular bandleaders in jazz history and his band, the Thundering Herd, helped define the musical form that became known as progressive swing.

Woodrow Charles Herman was born in May 1913 in Wisconsin. Even as a child he sang in vaudeville shows, and by the age of 14 was proficient on both saxophone and clarinet. He started as a bandleader in 1936 and from then on he led a series of top-rated bands right through the days of swing and into the era of rock 'n' roll. Although he was a gifted clarinettist, this talent was always overshadowed by his prowess as a bandleader, and although he toured and recorded with his big band for more than 50 years, he kept the sound fresh and promoted the talents of many of jazz's greatest musicians.

The Herd popularised now-classic songs such as "Blues on Parade", "Blue Prelude", "The Woodchopper's Ball", "Bijou" and "Beau Jazz". The band also appeared in a number of Hollywood movies, most notably *New Orleans* and *The Hit Parade of 1947*. Herman always allowed the newer and younger musicians to bring their influences into the band's repertoire. For example, during the 1970s the band was playing jazz rock and soul rock. Because of Herman's amiable personality, he had a fine rapport with all the musicians he worked with and gained great respect for his work in other fields of music, such as rock, classical and country.

Herman remained active until his health declined in 1986 and he died a year later in Los Angeles.

Above: Woody Herman.

COOL JAZZ ERA (1944–1970)

BEBOP

The 40s marked the birth of bebop, which became the foundation of modern jazz. The war years had caused many swing musicians to go into military service, reducing the number of players in bands to quartets and quintets. This helped younger talents get their breaks and gain access to the venues. Whereas jazz styles prior to this had placed the emphasis on tunes that could be hummed or danced along to, bebop put the emphasis on technique, moving jazz onto a mathematic and academic level. This sort of jazz was no longer the music of the masses; rather it gathered an elitist following of intellectuals and fellow musicians and its enjoyment was simply centred on the satisfaction of the musicians themselves. Indeed, some of the bandleaders from the swing era reacted in a very hostile manner to the new sound.

Many of the personalities associated with bebop were volatile young men, who started off outside the mainstream. Musicians became artists, using the notes to form landscapes of sound. Instead of relying on musical conventions they created new styles and emphasised technique. Hard-to-play fast tempos and eighth-note runs abounded in bebop, pushing the technical skills of the musician into the future. An intricate melody would normally be played, followed by a solo based on chordal instead of melodic improvisation, and often the melody was left behind altogether.

The man deemed to be the father of the tenor saxophone, and was there for the birth of bebop, was Coleman Hawkins. Although he started his career in the 1920s, he managed to remain an innovator throughout the whole of his career by rolling with the changes that happened in jazz. He was a major influence on the players of this new style.

BIOGRAPHY:
Coleman Hawkins

Saxophone

Coleman "Hawk" Hawkins was born in Missouri in 1904. He was a child prodigy in the area of music and was discovered playing in a theatre orchestra pit in Kansas City by the blues singer Mamie Smith. After playing with her Jazz Hounds for a year, he went on to play first with Wilbur Sweatman and then the Fletcher Henderson Orchestra in 1924.

It was his deep and melodic tone, in contrast to the usual percussive style of vaudeville-based jazz players, that gave him his edge and influences other saxophonists after him. He played and recorded with the Henderson orchestra for ten years, although he also worked with several other bands in the studio. In 1934 he moved to Europe and recorded with jazz guitarist Django Reinhardt among others. In 1939 he played with the Jack Hylton Orchestra in England but, with the outbreak of World War II, decided to return to the States. In 1940 he recorded his most famous record, "Body and Soul", which is now regarded as a jazz standard.

In the 1940s Hawkins adapted to bebop. He hired a number of young musicians, who were soon to be legends, for his bands, such as Thelonius Monk, Dizzy Gillespie and Miles Davis. By the 1950s his style, in comparison to the likes of Lester Young and Charlie Parker, seemed outmoded. However, Hawkins adapted yet again and recorded with Thelonius Monk and the likes of John Coltrane, Duke Ellington and Sonny Rollins. He remained at the forefront of jazz right up until his death in 1969.

Leading the vanguard of bebop was the alto saxophonist Charlie "Bird" Parker who, along with his primary accomplices Dizzy Gillespie and Miles Davis, was to change forever the sound of jazz. His style allowed him to fully express himself through his playing.

Above: Coleman "Hawk" Hawkins.

BIOGRAPHY:
Charlie Parker

Saxophone

Charlie Parker was born in Kansas City, Missouri, in August 1920. He learned to play alto sax at the age of 11 and played at night in the local clubs. He was considered something of a young upstart as his skills were somewhat lacking, but his enthusiasm was boundless.

At the age of 16 he learned a different style of playing the saxophone from a guitarist friend, which involved weaving melodies into the chords. He also learned more musical theory. Sadly, he had developed a drug addiction by this age and ended up going to jail, leaving his saxophone behind.

Parker eventually moved to New York City where he played in a few clubs, borrowing the saxes from other musicians. Eventually he was bought a sax by unknown parties, obviously curious to see what he could do with his own. By the end of 1939 Parker was about to find his own style of bop. One of his colleagues at that time, Biddy Fleet, said: "Charlie suddenly found that by using higher intervals of a chord as a melody line and backing them with appropriately related changes, he could play this thing he had been hearing in his mind but had previously been unable to play".

In the 1940s Parker worked with Earl Hines, alongside Dizzy Gillespie and Billy Eckstine. None of this band's output was recorded due to a strike at the time. He played the tenor sax but in 1944 swapped back to alto when he joined Eckstine's band. Unfortunately, the band was met with hostility at times which led to

problems with Parker who would get depressed. It was at this time that Parker was to record his famous Dial sessions, which feature some of the best examples of early bop there are. His cohorts from the Eckstine band also featured on these recordings. He returned to New York in 1947, forming a quintet which was to perform many of his best-known songs. In 1949 he toured around Europe and recorded an album using strings in the background. In 1950 the Birdland club was also opened in honour of him.

In the 1950s Parker's personal life began to take a downturn. This also affected his professional life. His New York cabaret licence was revoked in 1951, making it hard for him to play in clubs. In 1954 one of his daughters died of pneumonia. He was battling a drinking problem as well as trying to stay off drugs, and attempted suicide twice. In March 1955, after making his final public appearance at Birdland, Parker died of unknown causes in the apartment of his close friend, Baroness Pannonica de Koenigswater, after having been ill for several days.

Baroness de Koenigswater, known as Nica, was a patron to many of the jazz musicians in New York and would help them out in times of need. Her apartment had an open-door policy and she held regular meetings there. Another of her close friends was Thelonius Monk, whom she had met in Paris in 1954. Monk was renowned for both his intensity and the way he used humour in his music.

Above: Charlie Parker recorded some of the best examples of early bop.

BIOGRAPHY:

Thelonius Monk

Piano

Thelonius Sphere Monk was born in October 1917 in North Carolina. His family moved to Manhattan early in his childhood. He started playing the piano at the age of five and after receiving formal instruction in his early teens began to play at local churches and theatres.

He excelled in his academic life at school, but because of segregation issues was unable to join the school band. In 1935 he left school and pursued a career as a pianist for an evangelist who toured around doing faith healing. In 1941, having played in a number of small bands, he was hired by the drummer Kenny Clarke to play at Minton's Playhouse, Harlem. It was here that many other bebop musicians mingled and met for after-hours jam sessions in the clubs in the vicinity. He was to meet Charlie Parker, Dizzy Gillespie, and Bud Powell amongst others.

His wonderfully harmonic compositions such as "52nd Street Theme" and "I Mean You", combined with his economic playing style, meant he was a major contributor to the early development of modern jazz. He utilised both hands equally in his playing, over the whole keyboard, but graciously left plenty of space for his fellow musicians to improvise their own solos.

In 1944 Monk was hired by Coleman Hawkins to record with him for the small record label Blue Note. In 1947 Monk had the opportunity to lead his own recording sessions, working with top musicians of the day. Sadly the records were met with hostility by the critics at the time which meant he struggled to find work. This was further exacerbated when, in 1951, he was arrested for possession of drugs (he covered for his friend Bud Powell) which meant he lost his licence to work the clubs in New York. Fortunately, he was still able to record and compose, and over the next few years performed alongside Miles Davis and Sonny Rollins.

In 1954 he travelled to Europe for the first time to play at the Paris Jazz Festival. This helped establish his imaginative style of playing and from there on his career began to flourish. His licence to play New York clubs was reissued in 1957 and he had the opportunity to lead big bands for large audiences. Monk was very much a family man and because of his tendency to stay at home whilst not working he earned the title of eccentric recluse.

In the 1960s he put together a quartet which went on world tours and recorded a number of best-selling albums such as *Monk's Dream*. By the late 60s his health had begun to fail, so he worked fewer and fewer assignments. His last public engagement was in 1976.

In February 1982, following a stroke, Monk died at the house of Nica (Baroness De Koenigswater), with his wife at his bedside.

Above: Thelonius Monk — the High Priest of Bebop.

COOL JAZZ

Cool jazz is a style that emphasises the composer and arranger in its complex harmonies, overlaid by solos. It is heavily influenced by classical music and features arrangements which are more intricate than regular bebop.

Although Miles Davis first appeared on the bebop recordings of Charlie Parker, it was his first session as bandleader that led to *Birth of the Cool* which is deemed to be the first cool jazz album. Davis developed improvisational techniques utilising modes, rather than standard chord changes. His musical experimentation changed the sound of jazz and left a legacy of jazz standards through his inspirational chill-outs.

BIOGRAPHY:
Miles Davis

Trumpet

Miles Dewey Davis was born in Illinois in May 1926. He grew up in St Louis and it was there that he first learned the trumpet at the age of 13 and performed around his neighbourhood. It was when he went to see Billy Eckstine's band playing that he met Charlie Parker and Dizzy Gillespie. In 1945 Davis went to Juilliard School of Music in New York and was soon performing in bands alongside the likes of Charlie Parker and Coleman Hawkins. He left the school, preferring instead to learn by jamming in clubs on 52nd Street in Manhattan.

In 1946 Davis toured around Los Angeles and recorded with Charlie Parker. He linked up with Billy Eckstine's band but eventually moved back to New York in 1947. That same year he recorded again with Charlie Parker but also led his own band, the Miles Davis Allstars, with whom he recorded. In 1948 he once again played in Parker's groups.

It was in 1949 that the first *The Birth of The Cool* sessions were recorded, featuring a nine-piece band including Gerry Mulligan, J J Johnson and Lee Konitz. Further sessions followed in 1950 and it was during this period that Davis developed a more relaxed playing style which was to become his signature until the mid-60s.

In the mid-1950s Davis recorded a number of albums featuring Sonny Rollins, Thelonius Monk and Charles Mingus amongst others. He also featured John Coltrane for the first time, as part of a new quintet.

The 1960s saw Davis work with a new rhythm section, featuring the innovative Herbie Hancock amongst others. From 1965 – 1968 the Davis quintet was amazingly influential on the likes of Wynton Marsalis as it bridged the gap between free jazz and hard bop.

After 1968 and through the early 1970s, Davis turned onto rock jazz and utilised guitars, keyboards and electronic effects on his trumpet. Although many of his recordings at the time were of a commercial nature, much of the onstage jams his ensembles performed were extremely intense. The album *Bitches Brew* in 1969 saw the birth of jazz rock fusion and has continued to be a standard ever since.

In 1975 Davis retired. His recreational drug use had adversely affected his health and it was not until 1981 that he was able to work again. Throughout the 1980s he toured, changing from the 1970s rock sound to a more funky pop sound. He played the Montreux Jazz Festival in the summer of 1991. Sadly this was his last major performance as he died in September 1991.

Another influential musician and principal mover of the cool style was Lester Young, whose long career encompassed swing, alongside the likes of Count Basie and Billie Holiday, before his melodic style revolutionised jazz into bebop. His inspirational style of combining light sounds with alternative fingerings in order to create a dark, bluesy tone means that many saxophonists have sought to emulate him since. He

epitomised cool as he was a "snazzy" dresser, had his own style of speech and also held the saxophone almost horizontally when he played.

Above: Miles Davis – King of Cool.

BIOGRAPHY:

Lester Young

Saxophone

Lester Willis Young was born in Missouri in August 1909. As a child he played drums in his father's minstrel band but in 1927 he switched to the tenor saxophone. After leaving the family band he went and played with a number of bands in clubs before moving in 1933 to Kansas City, where he joined the Bennie Moten Band. He then played with King Oliver, Fletcher Henderson and in 1934 with the Count Basie band. In doing so, he helped to put Kansas City on the map of jazz history. In 1936 he rejoined the Basie band for recording and touring and remained with them for four years. It was during this time that Young earned the nickname "The Prez" from Billie Holiday.

In the 1940s he moved to Los Angeles and played with a number of small bands. In 1944 he was drafted but at this point his personal life and career took a turn for the worse as he was arrested for possession of marijuana and spent his military life in prison. He was never to recover from this and his playing and personality became erratic. When he played in the late 1950s with Miles Davis he received bad reviews which was to further knock his confidence.

He died after complications caused by alcoholism in 1959.

One of the main musicians on *The Birth of Cool* album was Gerry Mulligan.

BIOGRAPHY:

Gerry Mulligan

Saxophone

Gerry Mulligan was born in April 1927 in New York. Although he was best known as the master of the baritone saxophone, he was a multi-instrumentalist and also made jazz piano recordings. He was a prolific composer and experimenter and worked with as many styles of jazz as the number of instruments he was able to play.

Mulligan was a very gregarious musician, much quoted and often in the headlines. He associated with such jazz greats as Gene Krupa, Miles Davis, Stan Kenton, Dave Brubeck, Thelonius Monk and many others.

Mulligan died in January 1996 following complications from knee surgery.

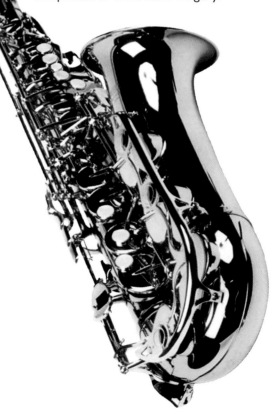

AFRO-LATIN JAZZ

The history of Afro-Latin music goes back to the 1910s when the tango was first introduced into Europe and the USA. New Orleans jazz combined both African polyrhythms and the rhythms of South and Central America which had come from the Spanish, Portuguese and French immigrants who had been living there for centuries. It was not long, therefore, before the fusion of Latin rhythms with jazz set the stage for some extremely creative performances from the likes of Dizzy Gillespie who was another innovator of bebop, particularly in the sub genre of cool jazz.

Above: Dizzy Gillespie, an innovator of bebop.

BIOGRAPHY:

Dizzy Gillespie

Trumpet

John Birks "Dizzy" Gillespie was born in October 1917 in South Carolina, the youngest in a family of ten. His father was a bandleader and accordingly encouraged him to learn instruments early on. He first learned to play the piano, then the trombone, but switched to trumpet. In 1935, following a music scholarship, he began his career, working his way around a number of bands before earning a place with Cab Calloway for two years until 1941, when he was fired after an onstage incident which ended up in a fight between the bandleader and Gillespie. It was during this time that Gillespie first began to take an interest in Afro-Cuban music which was to greatly influence his playing.

Over the next few years he worked with more bands, including those of Duke Ellington, Ella Fitzgerald and Coleman Hawkins. During this time he met Charlie Parker, who became a lifelong friend. He also met Thelonius Monk at clubs such as Minton's Playhouse and the pair began to experiment. When, in late 1942, Dizzy and Charlie Parker played in Earl Hines's band, Bebop was born, with the song "Night in Tunisia". The first bebop big band was created when Billy Eckstine, Gillespie, Sarah Vaughan and Charlie Parker left Earl Hines in the mid-1940s.

As his popularity increased Gillespie also sought an outlet for his interest in Afro-Cuban music and he was able to experiment with it for the rest of his life.

In 1953 his trumpet was accidentally bent by being sat upon. Gillespie liked the sound so much that he had all his trumpets custom-made with the bend from then on.

In October 1992, on his 75th birthday, Gillespie was booked to play at his favourite club, the Blue Note Jazz Club in New York. It was to be his last appearance there as he died from cancer in January 1993.

Above: Dizzy Gillespie and his famous bent trumpet.

BIOGRAPHY:

Stan Getz

Saxophone

Stan Getz was born in February 1927 in Philadelphia. He started to learn to play instruments from an early age and by the age of 12 was proficient on the harmonica. He was picked for his school band in which he played bass, but at the age of 13 he was bought an alto sax. After trying different saxophones he found that it was the sound of the tenor sax that was his favourite.

He joined Jack Teagarden's band in 1943 and the following year Stan Kenton, followed by Jimmy Dorsey in 1945 and Benny Goodman in 1946. From 1947 to 1949 he joined Woody Herman's Herd.

In the 1950s Getz joined the cool jazz movement, playing with bebop but in a very subtle manner. He played alongside the likes of Gerry Mulligan, Lionel Hampton and Oscar Peterson. However, in 1954 he was imprisoned for using drugs and, in order to escape the social scene surrounding his addictions, moved to Denmark for a number of years. In 1961 he returned to America and joined the Brazilian composer Antonio Carlos Jobim and Joao and Astrud Gilberto, helping to make the bossa nova sound more popular. In 1963 he recorded "The Girl from Ipanema" which had great international success and is considered a jazz standard. In 1967 Chick Corea joined to make the band a quintet. In 1969 in order to overcome further drug problems, Getz moved to Malaga in Spain and it was not until 1971 that he started performing again. He made over 300 recordings in his life.

Getz died from cancer in 1991.

Bossa nova is a blend of jazz and the samba rhythms of Brazil.

Above: In 1963 Stan Getz recorded "The Girl from Ipanema" which had great international success and is considered a jazz standard.

HARD BOP

Hard bop was a style developed in the 1950s which placed less emphasis on the technical melodies of bebop. Instead, the style maintains the rhythmic intensity of bebop but brings in more blues and gospel melodies. The general public appreciated the opportunity to participate once again in jazz performances. This style reached back into the hot jazz era that had been abandoned by the cool style and reclaimed jazz as a predominantly Afro-American expression. Hard bop uses simpler harmonies with easily recognisable tunes, and an emphasis on rhythms; it is exemplified particularly in the performances of Art Blakey and Cannonball Adderley.

BIOGRAPHY:
Art Blakey

Drums

Art Blakey was born in October 1919 in Pittsburgh, Pennsylvania. He learned piano at school and played in the school band. He then taught himself to play drums by listening to records, particularly those of Chick Webb, and from there on remained with this instrument.

In 1943 and 1944 he toured with the Fletcher Henderson Orchestra throughout the southern states of America, and then joined Billy Eckstine's new band. It was during this time from 1944 to 1947 that he met many of the cool jazz pioneers, including fellow band member Miles Davis. After the Eckstine band broke up, he organised a band and began recording with this octet under the name of the Jazz Messengers. The Jazz Messengers were the training ground for many of the most prolific soloists in jazz history. In the late 1940s he travelled to Africa to learn more about the culture and the music of Islam, the religion he would eventually convert to.

During the 1950s he performed and made radio broadcasts with Charlie Parker, Miles Davis, Clifford Brown and Horace Silver. In February 1954, working with a quintet, featuring Lou Donaldson on sax and Clifford Brown (trumpet), he recorded the "Night at Birdland" gig which became world-famous. This quintet was so successful that they made the line-up permanent and continued with the name The Jazz Messengers. Throughout the various line-ups, the Jazz Messengers have always had strong trumpet players that Blakey used as a percussive element.

During the early 60s the Jazz Messengers began to work with the soul jazz style and many young musicians, such as Wayne Shorter, Wynton Marsalis and Keith Jarrett would cut their teeth with the band. Blakey also recorded with Thelonius Monk, the Modern Jazz Quartet, John Coltrane and various African and Latin jazz groups.

From 1971 to 1972 he joined a world tour with the Giants of Jazz. He also frequently appeared at the Newport Jazz Festival. Blakey was most certainly a major figure in shaping modern jazz style and was one of its greatest talent scouts and mentors. As a drummer he played extraordinary solos which helped define the sound of hard bop. Towards the end of his career, Blakey organised drum sessions which included multiple drummers and African musicians and, although he was a loud and dominant drummer, he was also gracious enough to listen to his fellow band members.

He died as Abdullah Ibn Buhaina, his Islamic name, in New York in October 1990.

The man whose material walked a fine line between jazz and pop, Cannonball Adderley played solos vigorously and with great emotion. His tones were warm and his phrasing was lyrical. He incorporated Latin, African, gospel and blues elements into his arrangements.

Above: Art Blakey, though a loud and dominant drummer, was gracious enough to listen to his fellow band members.

BIOGRAPHY:

Cannonball Adderley

Saxophone

Julian Edwin Adderley was born in Florida in 1928. He was first called "Cannibal" because of his healthy appetite which then changed to "Cannonball". He was encouraged to enjoy music from an early age by his father, who was a teacher.

He started to play alto sax in local Floridian bands and became a high school band director. From 1950 to 1953 he served with the US Army and played in military bands. After he was discharged he decided to take up teaching as a career. However, in 1955 he moved to New York to play with his brother Nat and was an immediate success on the local jazz scene because of his fluid solos. The Adderley Brothers formed a quintet in 1956. He worked with Miles Davis from 1957 until 1959 and recorded on albums such as *Milestones*. Adderley also learned a great deal from Miles about using space within his solos during this time. In 1958 he made his most famous record *Something Else* which included both Davis and Art Blakey.

After playing on Davis' *Kind of Blue* album, alongside John Coltrane, Cannonball reformed his own quintet, including his brother Nat. In 1962 the group expanded to a sextet with the addition of tenor saxophonist Yusef Lateef. Later that year they recorded with the singer Nancy Wilson, and their albums continued to meet with great success into the 1970s. Adderley also led jazz workshops at colleges and universities in order to motivate young musicians and to educate the public on jazz music.

He died of a stroke in August 1975.

Although Dave Brubeck is a classically trained pianist with a laid-back style, he is seen as a highly controversial figure in jazz history. Amongst other unorthodox concepts, he introduced many unusual time signatures into his compositions, related more to classical constructs than jazz. However, some of his works have sold well into the millions and thus have introduced jazz to a younger audience.

Above: Cannonball Adderley.

BIOGRAPHY:

Dave Brubeck

Piano

Dave Brubeck was born in California in December 1920. He trained in classical music and piano as a child and by his early teens had already started to play in a local jazz band. He went to study music and composition at college and led a 12-piece band there.

In World War II Brubeck led a military band and, upon leaving service, resumed his musical studies. In 1948 he formed the Jazz Ensemble which went on to record as the Dave Brubeck Octet. In 1949 he formed a trio with a vibraphonist and bassist. In the late 50s this band was to become a quartet, with whom Brubeck performed some amazing college campus gigs and recordings such as "Take Five" from the album *Time Out*. His classic line-up would remain together until 1967 when Brubeck decided to devote all his time to composing. He has composed cantatas, musicals and ballets.

In the 1980s he resumed working with quartets again and has toured around the world and received numerous accolades and awards. He continues to compose to this day.

BRUBECK

Above: Dave Brubeck, composer and musician.

WORLD FUSION

World fusion is ethnic music from any non-Western culture, mixed in with the various styles of jazz. There is, for example, Cuban jazz, Brazilian jazz, North African jazz, Polynesian jazz, Indian jazz and Caribbean jazz. Django Reinhardt melded the traditions of gypsy music and French concert music with jazz during the 1930s. John McLaughlin's music, particularly during the 70s and 90s, drew heavily on traditions from India. Sun Ra's music from the 1950s into the 1990s used even more African rhythms.

Caribbean dance rhythms have always played a significant part in American popular music throughout the 20th century. Many jazz musicians, have visited and played in the Caribbean and brought back their own variations on reggae. World fusion jazz is a continuum as more and more cultures collide, particularly on the Internet which allows musicians from many parts of the world to play together in cyberspace, without even meeting.

One of the most talented exponents of world fusion music is Keith Jarrett. Dizzy Gillespie's "A Night in Tunisia", recorded by Keith Jarrett's quintet, brought in Middle Eastern instrumentations and harmonics.

BIOGRAPHY:
Keith Jarrett

Piano

Keith Jarrett was born in May 1945 in Pennsylvania. He was born into a musical family. He first learned the piano at the age of three and had a classical music education throughout his childhood, studying composition as well. At the age of five he won first prize in a radio programme directed by Paul Whiteman. In his late teens he moved to Boston to study at the Berkley School of Music and then moved to New York where he joined the jazz scene there. In the late 1960s he formed a trio which soon became a quartet after tenor saxophonist Dewey Redman was added to the line-up.

In the early 1970s Jarrett was to play piano and organ alongside Miles Davis but since then Jarrett has always led his own bands. He also has a career as a solo pianist and has released many concert recordings, not only of his own compositions but of classical ones, too. Many of his own compositions have been premiered in important music centres around Europe and the States such as Paris, Vienna and Carnegie Hall.

Since 1983 Jarrett's jazz playing has been focused on playing American standards of the 30s, 40s and 50s as part of a trio with Gary Peacock (bass) and Jack De Johnette (drums). In 1988 he began work on a Bach/Jarrett keyboard cycle and in the 1990s he recorded Shostakovich's *Preludes and Fugues* opus 87 as well as pieces by Mozart. Jarrett has a large classical repertoire and has performed with

orchestras all over the world. Yet he still manages to incorporate a cascade of other styles within his music. Although he had a battle with Chronic Fatigue Syndrome which left him incapacitated for a time, he continues to be a successful composer and recording artist to this day.

Don Cherry played with many of the greats of the cool jazz era. Much of world fusion relies on not only ethnic sounds but the use of ethnic instruments. Don Cherry ensured the authenticity of the world fusion jazz by actively collecting instruments from a variety of cultural sources.

Above: Since 1983 Keith Jarrett's jazz playing has been focused on playing American standards of the 30s, 40s and 50s as part of a trio.

BIOGRAPHY:

Don Cherry

Trumpet/Multi-instrumentalist

Don Cherry was born in Oklahoma City in 1936. His family moved to Los Angeles and it was there, as a child, that he studied dance and piano. His father worked as a bartender in a top jazz club, enabling Cherry to listen to the best jazz players from a young age. He first studied the cornet in the late 1940s, whilst still in his teens, and it became his main instrument as he worked with the likes of Dexter Gordon and Red Mitchell.

In 1956 Cherry met up with Ornette Coleman and began to play in his bands. Together they worked on a whole new concept of jazz improvisation, making classic recordings such as *The Shape of Jazz to Come*. Although they were often met with hostility for their radical sound, it was not long until they gained an engagement at the Five Spot Club in New York. This launched the sound of free jazz, along with their 1960 album of the same name. After this was released Cherry was hired by Sonny Rollins and John Coltrane amongst others.

In 1963 Cherry was the co-founder of the New York Contemporary Five, which allowed him to tour on an international level. It was through his travelling that he acquired a taste for the music of the various countries he visited, soaking up the sounds and the ambience in his nomadic style. He started to promote what was to be called "world music", playing the different instruments he had picked up along the way at jazz festivals. In line with the protest music of the time he formed the Liberation Music Orchestra.

In 1970, Cherry left the USA because the political climate of the Vietnam War was incompatible with his beliefs. He moved to Sweden and set up an organic farm and a children's theatre with his wife and family. He was to introduce his theatre program into schools, both in Sweden and later on in the USA, when he had returned there in the 1980s. Throughout he emphasised jazz music and taught children how to make their own instruments.

Throughout the mid- to late 1970s, Cherry worked with his associates from the Coleman band again and also made a number of recordings which fused ethnic music with jazz.

Cherry died in October 1995.

Above: The multi-talented Don Cherry.

FREE JAZZ

Free jazz, as a term, came into being during the 1960s. As music it does not follow the usual guidelines of a pre-determined melody, tempo or chord progression and as such gives more spontaneity in terms of improvisation. To many, free jazz seems to be highly energetic, random group turbulence and can seem atonal due to the lack of chord progressions. However, to aficionados it is an exciting form of modern music that liberates the musician from the usual conventions of jazz.

The major proponent of free jazz was Ornette Coleman who, along with Cecil Taylor, Albert Ayler and their disciples, performed in this active and complex style of jazz. The man who claimed to have invented it, though, was Sun Ra, a larger-than-life character who stands out as the most eccentric jazzman ever.

BIOGRAPHY:

Sun Ra

Keyboards

Little can be confirmed about Sun Ra's origins. He was born in 1914 in Alabama. However, Ra insisted that he was from the planet Saturn. He may have been originally named Sonny Lee or Herman Blount.

Ra first started off being influenced by the blues as sung by Bessie Smith. In the 1930s he began to compose, arrange and play the piano. In 1946 he had moved to Chicago and began to play piano for the Fletcher Henderson Orchestra, as well as write arrangements. In 1948 he was to work with Coleman Hawkins and Eugene Wright's Dukes of Swing.

The 1950s saw Ra start his own band. The Arkestra were a ten-piece experimental group who were to stay together for over 30 years, albeit under different names. They played an unusual form of bebop and experimented with electronic keyboards and polyrhythmic percussion. Owing to this, Ra often claimed that he created free jazz. Ra had his own record label, Saturn, and was therefore one of the first musicians to own his own label.

In the 1960s the Arkestra and Ra moved first to New York and then to Philadelphia. Although they made many albums, the band still had no money and because of this they lived together in a commune. Ra had strict rules for his musicians, such as no drugs and no alcohol, and he would make them practise at all hours of the day and night. Ra called his musicians "tone scientists" and would emphasise the infinite notes

between notes. The band also dressed up in space gear or ancient Egyptian costumes, accompanied by light effects and chanting. Sadly this meant that Ra was not taken seriously as a musical force.

In the 1970s Ra was to stress the importance of the African origins as well as the mystical dimensions of jazz music. He blended different styles of music at his concerts and recorded some solo piano albums, which showed the influence of Count Basie.

Sun Ra died in 1993.

Above: Sun Ra — the Spaceman of Jazz.

BIOGRAPHY:

Ornette Coleman

Saxophone

Ornette Coleman was born in 1930 in Fort Worth, Texas. In 1944 he taught himself music and learned to play the saxophone, having been predominantly influenced by Charlie Parker, and went on to form his first band in 1945. His interests besides music lay in the fields of physics, mathematics and chemistry and he sought to capture this within his music.

In 1948 he moved to New Orleans to work at regular jobs, rarely playing music. In the early 1950s he moved to Los Angeles and worked with Pee Wee Crayton's rhythm-and-blues band. Sadly, whenever he tried to introduce his own style he was met with hostility. He left music performance briefly and began to study music theory on his own, using his own interpretations to further evolve his concept of the way he wanted to play. By 1958 he was playing around some of the clubs in Los Angeles, using his own style, and made his first studio recording after he had come to the attention of Percy Heath of the Modern Jazz Quartet.

In 1959 Coleman attended the Lenox School of Jazz in Massachusetts, after which he played at the Five Spot nightclub in New York and made further recordings which were released as two albums – *The Shape of Jazz to Come* and *Change of the Century*. In certain circles these were met with great criticism because of his unconventional style. In 1961 he released his album *Free Jazz* which contained a 37-minute long improvisation.

In 1962 Coleman retreated from the public eye in order to teach himself to play the trumpet and the violin. When he re-emerged from his studies in 1965, he was once again met with criticism over his treatment of the instruments in his recordings. Through the mid- to late 1960s he recorded and toured in Europe which accepted his sound more readily than did the USA. He even composed and produced works for large ensembles.

In the 1970s Coleman went electric by mixing guitars into his work. He also fused the sounds of Morocco into his band's repertoire. He has continued to work throughout the decades since, recording with rock musicians and writing film soundtracks, all the while staying on the cutting edge of avant garde music.

Although Louis Armstrong and Charlie Parker are the best-known jazz soloists, the man who probably had the most significant influence on other jazz musicians is John Coltrane. He was the musicians' musician, albeit that his style was sometimes considered violent. In 1960 he released his album *The Avant-Garde* which delved into free jazz. Coltrane also recorded Ornette Coleman's "The Invisible" and was influenced by his style.

Above: Ornette Coleman.

BIOGRAPHY:

John Coltrane

Clarinet/Saxophone

John William Coltrane was born in North Carolina in September 1926. He was born into a religious family: his grandfather was a minister and both of his parents played music at the local church. As a child he learned to play both the clarinet and alto saxophone. He served in the US Navy in the early 1940s and played the clarinet in a military marching band. In 1945 he moved to Philadelphia and it was here that he began his career as a professional musician. In 1949 he joined Dizzy Gillespie's band until 1951 when he resumed his education for a year. In the early 50s he played with Earl Bostic, Johnny Hodges and even Charlie Parker.

In 1955 he swapped to the tenor saxophone and joined the original Miles Davis Quintet, who were to cut some of the most influential recordings of the time. He left in 1957 after being fired due to his erratic behaviour caused by his drug problem. He joined up with Thelonius Monk at New York's Five Spot club which stretched Coltrane's playing ability even further. He was assisted in beating his drug problem by staying in Sun Ra's commune which had a total ban on drink and drugs. It was here that he received a spiritual awakening. Coltrane returned to play with Davis in 1958 for two years. He played on the legendary *Milestones* and *Kind of Blue* albums, as well as his own sessions including *Giant Steps*.

On leaving Davis, Coltrane was to record *My Favorite Things* in 1961, on which he played soprano sax. This historic album was to inspire generations of saxophonists, with its overwhelming power and the attention paid to composition and arrangements. In 1962 records a number of albums including *Live at Birdland* and *Bye Bye Blackbird*. On 9 December 1964 he recorded *A Love Supreme* and from there on his music took on a very spiritual and religious orientation, harking back to his upbringing and the revelation he had received whilst detoxing from heroin and alcohol. He continued with this focus up until his death with compositions such as "Meditations" and "Om", blending an Eastern sound into his style.

Sadly, Coltrane died in July 1967 due to liver failure.

Above: John Coltrane – the Spirit of Jazz.

JAZZIN' IN THE UK

THE EARLY YEARS

Jazz began in the UK on 1 April 1919 when the Original Dixieland Jazz Band arrived in Liverpool. This band, at the height of their popularity in the States, were a completely new phenomenon to the British audiences and set the pattern for the next ten years during which many British bands would emulate their style. They played many gigs, particularly in London, and became famous for their "Darktown Strutters' Ball" and "Tiger Rag". They also recorded here for Columbia and these early records, when listened to, reveal their spirited improvisations on their own tunes. They opened at the London Hippodrome as part of the musical revue *Joy Bells*. Afterwards they toured variety theatres and finally settled at London's Hammersmith Palais de Danse for a stay of nine months. During the total of 15 months that they stayed in the UK, they also performed at Buckingham Palace for King George V and played at the Peace Ball at the Savoy Hotel. They returned to the USA in July 1920.

Another US band called the Southern Syncopated Orchestra also appeared before the Royal Family at Buckingham Palace. Sidney Bechet was one of the members of the orchestra; unfortunately, he was charged with attempted rape and, although he was acquitted, he was deported.

In January 1926, the *Melody Maker* newspaper was launched by Lawrence Wright, who was a songwriter. This was to popularise jazz music throughout the country. Its first record review was of a tune called "Araby" played by the Savoy Orpheans who were resident at the Savoy Hotel, London. Many top American bands toured Europe during this time, the most famous and popular being the Paul Whiteman Orchestra.

In July 1932 *Melody Maker* announced that Louis Armstrong was to visit the country. Armstrong's reputation had built up since his records had been released here and he was considered to be the greatest jazz master of the time. However, once he arrived, he received mixed audience reactions. The older members of the audience stormed out on many occasions, as they had no experience of the kind of trumpet playing that Satchmo specialised in. In fact, many of them considered that he did everything else with his trumpet except play it. For the younger members of the audience, though, Louis was their hero and his music was the "underground" music of the time.

Melody Maker itself had been praising his virtuosity and when Louis appeared at the London Palladium his genius was revealed. However, there was at this time still a great deal of prejudice against the "black man's music" and, whereas jazz played by white bands was happily accepted, "negro" music was unacceptable to many of the bigots of the time. So, despite the black bands being the masters of jazz, the critics were more likely to praise the white bands. Although Satchmo had packed houses on his tour, he made very little money and left behind him mixed feelings about his music.

When he finally left Europe for America in the spring of 1935, he must have realised for the first time that he was now accepted as not only a highly regarded jazz virtuoso but a celebrity as well. Much of this was due to *Melody Maker* itself, as well as the record companies which released his records when he was an unknown and, of course, the great enthusiasm of his supporters.

In 1933, Duke Ellington's famous orchestra arrived, enthralling the general public with a spectacle of 13 black men performing before their very eyes. Interweaving flights of improvisation with orchestral virtuosity, this highly imaginative and superbly executed distillation of Afro-American culture was a revelation to British audiences and an assault upon their senses.

In 1935 the Ministry of Labour announced that they would no longer grant permits for the Duke Ellington Orchestra or any other American band to play in Britain until satisfactory reciprocal arrangements were made with the American Federation of Musicians. Whist the ban was detrimental in some ways, it also meant that British jazz had a chance to flourish on its own merits.

In the meantime, in 1938 the Quintet of the Hot Club of France, starring Django Reinhardt and French violinist Stéphane Grappelli, toured the country. This band was Europe's contribution to the development of jazz during this time and Reinhardt is still viewed today as the all-time greatest jazz genius of guitar.

Above: The Quintet of the Hot Club of France, starring Django Reinhardt and French violinist Stéphane Grappelli.

BIOGRAPHY:

Django Reinhardt

Guitar

Jean Baptiste Reinhardt was born in Belgium in January 1910 to a gypsy family. He was given his first instrument at the age of ten and, after learning the violin, quickly picked up on the fingering of the guitar. He was soon performing alongside an accordionist at local Parisian dance halls and even made some recordings by accompanying other musicians.

Sadly in November 1928, he was burnt in a fire at his caravan. As a result, the fingers on his left hand were seared together and he very nearly lost his leg; the doctors felt the damage was so great he would need an amputation. Whilst recuperating in hospital, which lasted for over a year, he was given a guitar. He relearned to play the guitar by using his index and middle fingers to solo, as his other fingers were too badly damaged, thereby inventing a new chord technique. In 1930, having recovered from his injuries, he heard the jazz recordings of Louis Armstrong and Duke Ellington which had a profound influence on his creativity. Although he could not read or write, particularly music, he still managed to compose.

In 1934 his meeting with violinist Stéphane Grappelli resulted in the Quintet of the Hot Club of France. This band was to record hundreds of songs which were released both in Europe and in the USA. In 1938 the Quintet went to tour England. Owing to the outbreak of World War II, Grappelli remained in England but Reinhardt returned to Paris and stayed there to play his music, even throughout the Nazi occupation, a difficult task considering he was of gypsy extraction.

After the war he and Grappelli continued to play and record together. Reinhardt made a brief tour of the USA in 1946, playing with Duke Ellington, and it was on this tour that he first played an electric guitar. He then returned to Paris until his retirement in 1951. By 1952 he had settled down with his wife and two sons in Samois, near Paris but continued to travel frequently to concerts.

He died in May 1953.

Above: Django Reinhardt – the gypsy jazz guitarist.

BIOGRAPHY:
Jack Hylton

Piano

Jack Hylton was born in July 1892 in Lancashire. Physically only five foot three, he became a giant on the British music scene for some four decades. He started his career as "The Singing Mill Boy", playing piano at concert parties and working in a double act with Tommy Handley. He played with the Queen's Dance Orchestra at the Queen's Hall, London and they first recorded for HMV on 28 May 1921. He was the only member of the band who could read music and before long his name appeared on the label as director of the orchestra. His 1922 band had Bernard Tipping on trombone, Basil Wiltshire on drums, Bert Heath and Jack Raine on trumpet, an unlisted tenor sax, Chappie d'Amato on saxophone, Dick de Pauw on violin and Bert Bassett on banjo.

Hylton was influenced by Paul Whiteman and used him as a model for his orchestra. He concentrated his efforts on touring while occasionally appearing in several West End shows. By 1926, Jack Hylton and his Orchestra were well established and made their very first broadcast. They were never regular broadcasters on the BBC so their appearances on the air were greeted as occasions not-to-be-missed, and they were the first British band to be broadcast to the United States. In the late 1930s they appeared on commercial radio in the *Rinso Radio Revue* for recorded half-hour programmes. Hylton himself had the foresight to have his broadcasts recorded and stored in his archives.

Between 1927 and 1938 the band made 16 European tours and was extremely successful throughout Europe. In 1932, Hylton was awarded the French Legion of Honour for his services to music.

Jack was famous both for presenting symphonic concert arrangements and for his impressive stage effects. The band was strong vocally and included over the years such singers as Sam Browne, Pat O'Malley, Alice Mann, Denny Dennis, Hylton's sister Dolly Elsie, June Malo, Bruce Trent, and Dick Murphy as well as the vocal group that Jack discovered and took to Europe – the Swingtette. Out of the Jack Hylton band came such future bandleaders as Billy Ternent, Paul Fenoulhet, Chappie D'Amato, Jerry Hoey, Peter Yorke and Jack Jackson. His musicians were paid well in return for high standards.

Hylton organised visits to Britain by Duke Ellington, Louis Armstrong and others and in 1935 he set his sights on touring the USA. He secured a contract for 13 hour-long broadcasts in the US for the Standard Oil Company. The whole band set sail on 16 October and broadcast in mid-ocean. However, because of a ban on foreign musicians by the American Musicians' Federation, only Hylton, Ternent and his singers Pat O'Malley, Peggy Dell and six other performers were granted permission to work. An American band was formed, under Hylton's direction, to play and broadcast from the Drake Hotel in Chicago.

Hylton

In 1940, because most of his musicians went to join the armed forces, he disbanded and began to concentrate on his management activities. The band gave their farewell concert at the Paris Opera House. After the war, Hylton became a very successful impresario presenting shows such as *The Crazy Gang*, *Kiss Me Kate*, *Kismet* and *Camelot* to London audiences.

There were two occasions when Jack conducted again. On 12 October 1943, he conducted the Glenn Miller Orchestra in the 1936 concert arrangement of *She Shall Have Music* which was broadcast. In 1950 he conducted a reunited Hylton Orchestra, including vocalists Sam Browne and Bruce Trent, at the Royal Command Performance. He died in 1965.

Until 1955, live jazz was heard only from British musicians, the only exceptions being performances played by off-duty members of the US Forces visiting or stationed in Britain, who jammed with these British bands. By the time the Ministry of Labour ban was lifted, many of the greatest jazz musicians that America produced had died and a whole generation were denied seeing or hearing and being influenced by this unique bunch of musicians.

During the 40s and 50s Great Britain was into what was called the Golden Age of the Dance Band, with their bowing, beaming and frock-coated bandleaders waving their batons – Bert Ambrose, Jack Hylton, Jack Payne, Billy Cotton, Roy Fox, Lou Stone and many others. All of these bands employed jazz-minded sidemen and occasionally a "hot" arrangement was permitted. Unfortunately the jazz-loving public in Great Britain was not large enough to keep jazz profitable during these years and most jazz was heard in cellar clubs in London and the provinces and played by amateurs.

The first of these clubs was called the British Rhythm Club No 1, and it held its inaugural meeting in Regent Street, London W1 on 24 June 1933. *Melody Maker* happily gave this and the many other clubs that followed their unstinting support.

World War II was the catalyst for many social changes that came to be reflected in jazz, resulting in Great Britain producing the greatest number of accredited jazzmen outside the USA. Conscription reduced the size of the big orchestras and curtailed the dominance of their bandleaders. During the war, many of the stodgy arrangements were set aside and the liveliness of jazz suited the prevailing mood of desperate light-heartedness. The most active musicians to emerge in this changing climate were trumpeters Kenny Baker, Arthur Mouncey and Leslie Hutchinson, saxophonists Ronnie Chamberlain and Aubrey Franks, clarinettists Frank Weir and Harry Parry, drummers Jock Cummings and George Firestone and pianists Art Thompson and George Shearing.

BIOGRAPHY:

George Shearing

Piano

George Shearing was born in London in August 1919. He was the last of nine children and was born congenitally blind. After only four years of formal education at the Linden Lodge School for the Blind, his piano-playing skills enabled him to win a number of university scholarships. However, he turned these down in order to pursue playing in local pubs which was more lucrative.

In the 1930s he joined a band consisting entirely of blind people and also performed for the BBC. Fortunately he met the jazz critic Leonard Feather. Through his influence he was able to emigrate to New York in the late 1940s where he established his credentials and absorbed the emerging bebop form. It was there he wrote the song "Lullaby of Birdland", about the famous club, which became a jazz standard. In 1949 he formed the first of his quintets and made a number of recordings.

Shearing's playing style is known as "locked hands" wherein chord clusters are featured around right-hand melodies. Besides his legendary musical ability, he is also known for his tuxedo and "cool shades".

In 1949 he had his first international hit with the cover of "September in the Rain" and this resulted in him switching to a more popular style, away from pure jazz. Since then he has won Grammy awards, played in many different styles, including Latin, and composed hundreds of songs. Shearing is equally at home in small jazz clubs as he is in large concert halls. For his 80th birthday he played a sell-out concert in Birmingham Symphony Hall. He is a dream to play with for many a jazz musician or singer and still going strong in his eighth decade. He was presented with the OBE in 1997.

Above: George Shearing — equally at home in small jazz clubs as he is in large concert halls.

THE 1940s

In 1940 the BBC at last acknowledged that there was a demand for jazz by broadcasting the *Radio Rhythm Club* for half an hour a week. Its resident band was led by clarinettist Harry Parry. The band recorded 102 titles for Parlophone, under the name of the Radio Rhythm Club Sextet. In 1947, the *Radio Rhythm Club* became *BBC Jazz Club* and was produced by Mark White, who later put together two compilation albums of all the 78s that Decca recorded from the Rhythm Club sessions. It was called the *Scrapbook of British Jazz* and included performances by musicians such as Spike Hughes, Lou Stone, Jack Hylton, Nat Gonella, Harry Gold, George Chisholm, George Webb, Sandy Brown, George Melly, Wally Fawkes, George Shearing, Ken Colyer and Chris Barber.

By the middle of the late 1940s, revived Dixieland jazz was being played at jazz clubs throughout the country. Perhaps the most famous of these was George Webb's Dixielanders, comprising George Webb (piano), Wally Fawkes (clarinet), Reg Ridgen (trumpet), Owen Bryce (cornet), Eddie Harvey (trombone), Buddy Vallis (banjo) and Roy Wicks (drums). The band began at the District Rhythm Club No 130 at the Red Barn, Bexleyheath. This and the other revivalist jazz bands were attempting to break away from the formless jam sessions of the 40s and their insistent thump or stomp became the sound of the Trad craze of the 50s and 60s. Many of these bands

came up through the dance band championships that were held throughout the country. Most of these jazz bands were amateur bands because it was very hard to find work as professional jazz musicians, but gradually the general public began to flock to the Dixieland jazz clubs that were springing up across the UK.

One of the most impressive and significant of the British jazz scene musicians was Humphrey Lyttelton. He made his first appearance at the Hot Club of London on 18 January 1947.

BIOGRAPHY:

Humphrey Lyttelton

Trumpet

Humphrey Lyttelton was born at Eton College in May 1921. His father was a housemaster there and he received his education at Eton. He served during the war as an officer in the Grenadier Guards. In 1947 he joined George Webb's Dixielanders and a year later he formed his first jazz band, Humphrey Lyttelton and his Band, touring both the UK and Europe. In 1948 he played at the first International Jazz Festival in Nice where he played alongside legends such as Jack Teagarden, Earl Hines and Louis Armstrong.

In 1949 he first started recording, including accompanying Sidney Bechet and then releasing his own records. In 1956 Lyttelton's Bad Penny Blues became a Top 20 hit, the first jazz record to do so here in the UK.

In 1956 his band were to open for Louis Armstrong's Allstars' London concerts. In the late 1950s Lyttelton enlarged his band to an eight-piece and since then he has continued to play with his band. As well as broadcasting on the BBC, he works as a freelance journalist. Among his many awards are a Lifetime Achievement Award from the BBC Jazz Awards in 2001.

The Dixieland traditionalists hated bebop and the cool beboppers could not understand why some of the young traditional musicians were still playing old music. Louis Armstrong's description of bop as "one long search for the right note" was applauded by the traditionalists. The British defenders of bebop actively disliked the name that was attributed to their music and preferred to call it "modern", and indeed this was the name that eventually stuck.

During this time the clothes that you wore, when you went out to these clubs, indicated the jazz music you liked. The modernists were snappy dressers with short hair and were also involved in the beginnings of the drug culture. The traditionalists were beer guzzlers, and wore their hair and beards long (the two camps eventually led on to mods and rockers).

Record companies started to take up on this modern form of jazz and recordings were made by Johnny Dankworth, Steve Race and Ronnie Scott amongst others. In fact, Ronnie Scott's Club became, and still is, the heartland of modern jazz in the UK with the 100 Club in Oxford Street as the centre for traditional jazz and blues.

RONNIE SCOTT'S JAZZ CLUB

In early 1948, bebop jazz hit the UK when Dizzy Gillespie's recordings began to be released and many young British jazz musicians became attracted to the complexities of this idiom. They saw it as a challenge to their technical skills and bebop allowed them greater freedom of interpretation. Club 11 was formed in this year in Great Windmill Street, at Mac's Rehearsal Rooms. There were two interchangeable bands of ten musicians, with an eleventh musician consisting of the club's manager Harry Morris. The most well-known of these musicians was Ronnie Scott.

Ronnie Scott's Club was formed because after visiting New York, in the late 1940s, Ronnie Scott dreamed of opening his own jazz club in London. It finally materialised 12 years later on 30 October 1959 in Soho. On the opening night the Tubby Hayes Quartet played, along with Ronnie Scott and his business partner Peter King. At this time, because of the Ministry of Labour ban, British jazz lovers were missing out on modern American jazz music. The price of imported 78s was high so Ronnie Scott's Club made a huge difference. During the first two years of opening they booked the best of British jazz musicians but failed to get work permits for their American counterparts. However, they eventually managed to work out an exchange deal whereby the Tubby Hayes Quartet went off to play in New York and Zoot Sims was booked for a four-week residency at Ronnie Scott's in November 1961. Further guest appearances were to follow from other American musicians such as Roland Kirk, Stan Getz, Al Cohn, Benny Golson and Wes Montgomery.

This club was so successful that it soon became necessary to move to larger premises and in 1965 Ronnie Scott's re-opened in Frith Street. In 1968 the building next door was acquired, enabling Scott to extend and add an upstairs room where pop-type acts could be showcased. The new club opened in October 1968 with the Buddy Rich Band. Many bands have played Ronnie Scott's who do not fit the jazz category – Mark Knopfler, Paul Rodgers and Elkie Brooks, for example.

Owing to the club's worldwide reputation, it has also featured in many films, videos and TV programmes, along with BBC broadcasts from there. Scott received the OBE in 1991 for services to jazz. In 1996 Ronnie Scott died after several years of ill health.

Above: Ronnie Scott..

BIOGRAPHY:
Acker Bilk

TRAD JAZZ

Clarinet

By 1950 Britain stood on the brink of its first real jazz age. All types of jazz flourished and became a significant part of the pop music scene. What became known as trad jazz was the music that got into the charts.

Trad jazz was basically a British version of New Orleans Dixieland jazz and literally hundreds of young men formed almost identical bands, playing identical music. The bands consisted of trumpet, clarinet, trombone, banjo, piano, bass and drums and over the next few years became big business.

Three of the most famous bands associated with this phenomenon were Chris Barber, Kenny Ball and Acker Bilk.

Bernard Stanley Bilk was born in Somerset in January 1929. He learned to play the piano as a child but it was in 1948, whilst serving with the Royal Engineers, that he picked up the clarinet, the instrument he was to become famous for.

In 1954 Bilk joined Ken Colyer's Jazzmen but left in 1956 to form his own group, the Paramount Jazz Band. He and his band would dress up in Edwardian outfits, complete with waistcoats and Bilk's trademark bowler hat. He had his first major hit in 1960 with "Summer Set". In 1961 he was to have his most successful record to date with the TV theme "Stranger on the Shore", written for his daughter. This was also successful on the other side of the Atlantic.

When trad jazz became less popular during the 1970s, Bilk worked the cabaret circuits and again had chart success in 1976 with "Aria". He and his band continued to release singles and albums, well into the 1990s. Bilk has also guest-starred on other musician's records, such as those of Van Morrison and Chris Barber.

In the 90s Bilk went into retirement to paint and was awarded an MBE in 2001. He still does the occasional tour.

Other bands followed Acker Bilk's sartorial gimmickry; for example Dick Charlesworth and his band dressed as city gents and Bobby Mickleburg and his band dressed as Confederate soldiers.

However, the man known to trad jazz devotees as "The Guv'nor" is Ken Colyer. He was a mainstay of the British jazz scene for decades.

Above: Acker Bilk — the man with the bowler hat.

BIOGRAPHY:

Ken Colyer

Trumpet

Ken Colyer was born in April 1928 in Norfolk. He taught himself to play both guitar and trumpet.

Towards the end of World War II he joined the merchant navy and, after landing in New York, he toured the jazz clubs in "the Village". He was inspired by what he heard. When he returned to England he became a founding member of the legendary Crane River Jazz Band, which played Dixieland jazz. He left the Cranes in early 1951 and then rejoined the merchant navy where he jumped ship at Alabama, and took a Greyhound coach to New Orleans. In the Crescent City he jammed with a number of local legends, but unfortunately was arrested and jailed for over a month for illegal entry to the USA. He then fronted the band that was soon to become Ken Colyer's Jazzmen, a band which lasted almost 20 years, although its first line-up disbanded after a year. All former members of the first band went on to achieve jazz fame in their own right such as Chris Barber, Monty Sunshine, Acker Bilk and Lonnie Donegan.

During the 1950s and 1960s Ken Colyer had one of the most influential of all British trad jazz bands. He also brought the George Lewis Jazz Band to Europe on several occasions.

Colyer also owned his own record label and had his own club, Studio 51, in London's West End. Unfortunately illness forced him to disband the Jazzmen early in 1971. From this period onwards he toured Europe as a guest with various bands, who were either called the Allstars or Allstar Jazzmen. In 1985 he was reunited with Acker Bilk for a recording session which turned out to be his last.

He died in 1988 after a long battle with cancer.

Hundreds of clubs were formed during the 50s and 60s in pubs, working men's clubs, village halls and dance halls, and the university circuit was overrun with trad jazz bands. Running parallel with trad jazz, although not with the same degree of popularity, was the emerging style of modern jazz. Most of the clubs devoted to this style were in London. Johnny Dankworth was perhaps the most commercially successful of all the modern bands.

Above: During the 1950s and 1960s Ken Colyer had one of the most influential of all British trad jazz bands.

BIOGRAPHY:

Johnny Dankworth

Saxophone

John Dankworth was born in 1927. He learned the clarinet from an early age and by the age of 17 was studying at the Royal Academy of Music in London. His first great inspiration was Benny Goodman, but he heard Charlie Parker and switched over to saxophone in honour of his idol. In 1949 he was presented with the award of Musician of the Year, the first of many honours to come. In 1959 and 1960 he had two hit records with "Experiments with Mice" and "African Waltz". He also toured the USA for the first time in 1959, alongside the Duke Ellington Orchestra.

From the 1960s onwards he was to compose countless film, theatre and TV scores, including the theme for *The Avengers* series. He has worked as musical director for big names such as Ella Fitzgerald, Nat "King" Cole, Sophie Tucker and his wife Cleo Laine. He has also been commissioned to write music by the National Theatre and the Royal Shakespeare Company.

In 1970 he and his wife founded "The Stables", a centre dedicated to residential courses, concerts and master classes for musicians, as well as children's summer camps.

He is a Fellow of the Royal Academy of Music and has been awarded Honorary Doctorates, as well as being a CBE.

Above: Johnny Dankworth.

TODAY

I n 1954 the Musicians' Union in the UK at last agreed on a reciprocal deal with the American Federation of Musicians. Many American orchestras and bands began to tour the UK, including Duke Ellington, Count Basie, Louis Armstrong and the Modern Jazz Quartet. Jazz also gained acceptance with local authorities and could be heard in parks and local music festivals during the summer. Summer schools were formed for jazz tuition and the Arts Council gave grants to orchestras and concert promoters and towards the establishment of a permanent National Jazz Youth Orchestra. During the summer months in the 50s, 60s, and 70s aficionados could choose from a variety of festivals devoted entirely to jazz, the most notable of which were Beaulieu and Redcar. The record companies responded to the burgeoning interest in and awareness of jazz by releasing a flood of records. Many magazines were launched dedicated to the genre.

Today, jazz in the UK has its own nationwide radio station and there are bands, both traditional and modern, playing throughout the country at clubs and universities. Ronnie Scott's Club continues to thrive. Many of the older American jazz musicians are able to come over to perform and turn on a whole new generation of listeners to their music.

Above: Miles Davis had the ability to turn on young and old with his talent for moving with the times.

MODERN JAZZ ERA (1970–2004)

JAZZ ROCK FUSION

During the 1960s rock 'n' roll came to the forefront of popular music. It allowed for untrained musicians to form bands, and many of the highly technical jazz musicians began to incorporate rock 'n' roll into their music, particularly by importing rock's instruments, volume and stylistic delivery. The earliest notable fusion experimentation happened under the guidance of Miles Davis, particularly in his album *Bitches Brew*. In the 1970s the style was further developed by John McLaughlin, Chick Corea and Frank Zappa. The jazz rock fusion style offered a new virtuosity and a new technical approach to jazz which has now become common practice.

BIOGRAPHY:

Chick Corea

Keyboards

Armando Chick Corea was born in June 1941 in Massachusetts. His father was a musician and he learned to play piano at the age of four. By the age of 17 he was already playing Manhattan's jazz scene.

During the 1960s his lively competition style began to emerge and his first recording, named *Tones for Joan's Bones*, was made. He also played piano accompanying Stan Getz and Sarah Vaughan. In 1968 he joined the legendary Miles Davis who encouraged him to work using electric keyboards to create unusual sound effects. He was involved in the recording of the classic albums *Bitches Brew* and *In A Silent Way*.

In the early 1970s he formed his own experimental, avant garde group called Circle. This band pushed jazz beyond its established limits. He then teamed up with Flora Purim and her husband Airto and Joe Farrell to form the band Return to Forever,. The initial band was a softer samba-flavoured ensemble and was instrumental in making the Fender Rhodes electric piano one of the staples of contemporary music. After a couple of Return to Forever albums, in which he began working with a Moog synthesiser, and after hearing what John McLaughlin was doing, he decided to add electric guitar, first with Bill Conners and later with Al DiMeola.

After Flora and Airto had left the band in 1972, Return to Forever recorded such innovative albums as *Where Have I Known you Before*, *No Mystery* and *Romantic Warrior* and were rewarded with rock-star status and sold-out arenas.

During the 1980s he formed the Chick Corea Electrick Band and the Chick Corea Akoustic Band whose debut album went to No 1 in the US charts. He has continued to release albums, some as a piano soloist working with improvisations and others featuring standards. In 1992 he co-founded his own record label which focused more on creativity.

He continues to perform, and composes and records some of the most innovative and exciting pieces in the jazz genre today.

One of the most intense and exciting bands of the 1970s was the Mahavishnu Orchestra which was led by the jazz rock guitarist John McLaughlin. They took the world by storm with their mesmerising sound.

Above: Chick Corea.

BIOGRAPHY:

John McLaughlin

Guitar

John McLaughlin was born in January 1942 in Yorkshire. At the age of nine he was encouraged to play piano by his mother, a violinist. He picked up the guitar after hearing one of his older brothers listening to Muddy Waters and Leadbelly. During his teens he tuned in to the music of Miles Davis, Cannonball Adderley, Django Reinhardt, John Coltrane and classical composers such as Debussy. Outside of these influences he also listened to flamenco music.

In the 1960s McLaughlin was to contribute to the British blues revival playing along with Alexis Korner, Georgie Fame and Graham Bond. He then began to experiment and produced some of the most exciting, free-ranging jazz music at that time. In 1969 he went to America and worked with Miles Davis, collaborating on his albums *Bitches Brew* and *In A Silent Way*.

In 1970 McLaughlin became a disciple of the Indian guru Sri Chimoy and was deeply inspired by his meditations to form the Mahavishnu Orchestra with Rick Laird (bass), Jan Hammer (keyboard), Jerry Goodman (violin) and Billy Cobham (drums). The band played at outrageous volume using mountains of sound equipment on stage. McLaughlin used a double-necked guitar to play a rhythmic fusion of rock and Indian classical music based on lengthy riff figures. His first three albums with the orchestra were characterised by non-stop virtuosity, leaving the listener confused as to who was playing what. A clash of egos broke the band

up and a second line-up was formed. They recorded with the violinist Jean-Luc Ponty and the London Symphony Orchestra. McLaughlin also met Carlos Santana who was a fellow disciple of Chimoy; this resulted in the ecstatic *Love, Devotion and Surrender* album.

In the mid-70s McLaughlin moved closer to Indian music with his all-acoustic group called Shakti, playing a specially designed Gibson guitar that allowed him to bend the strings and create drone-like effects similar to a sitar. During the 80s he reformed the Mahavishnu Orchestra with Billy Cobham.

Nowadays, between guest appearances with international musicians, he is still composing and teaches new musicians using interactive technology, as well as remixing and remastering all his old material to CD.

Pat Metheny is a musician with his foundations deep in the roots of early jazz but who has managed to update the sound of early jazz by the use of modern technology. Originally trained in horn instruments, he plays the guitar with the same sense of rhythm and harmony associated with that group of instruments.

Above: John McLaughlin.

BIOGRAPHY:

Pat Metheny

Guitar

Patrick Bruce Metheny was born in August 1954 in Missouri. He was raised in a musical environment and started to learn both the trumpet and music theory early on in his childhood. It was during the 1960s that he started to listen to early rock music and also to John Coltrane. He soon picked up a guitar and taught himself to play in local bands. By 1968 he was working regularly with jazz bands in Kansas City and in 1974 finally made it onto the international jazz scene.

With the release of his first album *Bright Size Life* in 1975, he completely reinvented the traditional jazz guitar sound for a new generation. Over the years he has performed with artists as diverse as Ornette Coleman and David Bowie, Herbie Hancock and Steve Reich. Along with his keyboardist, Lyle Mays, he has been composing for almost 30 years. This partnership has been compared to that of Lennon and McCartney by both listeners and critics alike.

Metheny's body of work includes compositions for large orchestras as well as for solo guitar and ranges from classical to rock and jazz. He is also accomplished in the academic arena, becoming the youngest-ever teacher at the University of Miami when he was 18. In 1996 he received an Honorary Doctorate from Berkley School of Music. He has also held music workshops all over the world.

As a musical pioneer in the realm of electronic music, he was one of the first jazz musicians to treat the synthesiser seriously, by using the Synclavier as a composing tool. He has also developed several new types of guitars including the 42-string Pikasso guitar. Over the years he has won countless polls as Best Jazz Guitarist. He has also won a number of Grammy awards for a variety of categories. The Pat Metheny Group won an unprecedented seven consecutive Grammy Awards for seven consecutive albums. He has spent most of his life on tour and continues to be one of the brightest sparks in the jazz community. He has not only attained popularity as a musician but has received great acclaim from his critics and peers.

Above: Pat Metheny, one of the first jazz musicians to treat the synthesiser seriously.

NEOBOP

Neobop evolved during the 80s when a new generation of jazz players were looking for a new musical direction, away from the 70s free style of jazz. The new players were searching for the rhythmic and harmonic sophistication of the bebop era. Instrumentalists such as Wynton Marsalis, Jeff Watts and Kenny Kirkland established neobop as a viable new genre. At the same time, soul jazz became a sub-category of hard bop, with its bluesy, melodic concept and repetitive rhythmic lines, the form of hard bop known to the largest audiences. Jimmy Smith, Jimmy McGriff, Les McCann, Hank Crawford and Houston Person personified soul jazz with its urban, electrified style, mixed with orchestral flourishes.

In fact many people consider this genre as no more than a jazzed extension of rhythm and blues. This is the direction that this music took with such exponents as King Curtis, Junior Walker and the Allstars.

The style of soul jazz has also been linked to the Tamla Motown music of the 60s. Artists such as Nina Simone and Lou Rawls added to the vocal expression of this form of jazz and thereby created newer and younger audiences for jazz in general. These modern styles of jazz are constantly changing and evolving into newer and more accessible forms such as pop jazz, funk jazz, acid jazz and electronic jazz. These modern creative forms tend to be softer than the earlier bop derivatives, many of them fitting into the chill-out music genre.

Above: Kenny Kirkland helped to establish neobop as a viable new genre.

BIOGRAPHY:
Wynton Marsalis

Trumpet

Wynton Marsalis was born in 1961 in New Orleans into a family of musicians. He began to study the trumpet at the age of 12. Throughout high school he performed with local New Orleans marching jazz bands and classical orchestras. At the age of 18 he attended the Juilliard School in New York.

In 1980 he was to join with Art Blakey's Jazz Messengers and signed a record deal. Over the next two years he toured and recorded with Blakey and other leading jazzmen, including Herbie Hancock. Owing to his ability to play both classical and jazz he has received awards in both those genres. In 1982 he led his own quintet and

since then has performed with a variety of small groups, in the fields of both jazz and classical music.

Marsalis has recorded over 30 jazz and classical albums, combined with numerous guest appearances on many other albums. He has toured all over the world and has performed over 120 concerts a year for nearly two decades. He is well known for composing, particularly dance music, but has also written for ballets, films and television. He also enjoys teaching young musicians as well as giving speeches on the black musical heritage of jazz. In 1997 he won a Pulitzer Prize for his oratorio *Blood on the Fields*.

Above: Wynton Marsalis.

BIOGRAPHY:

Wayne Shorter

Saxophone

Wayne Shorter was born in August 1933 in New Jersey. He attended a music and arts high school and graduated as an art major. Towards the end of his teens he picked up the saxophone, and was greatly influenced by hearing a Thelonius Monk composition on the radio.

In 1956 he graduated from New York University and served with the US Army until 1958. After playing in several bands he joined the Jazz Messengers in 1959, becoming the musical director of the band. He stayed with the band until 1963 and a year later joined up with the Miles Davis Quintet, replacing John Coltrane With Davis he developed his playing style, as well as writing many songs which have since become jazz standards such as "Footprints".

In 1970 he formed his own band, Weather Report, which fused jazz with rock, classical and the emerging electronic music. Since then he has continued to compose and release albums, and has also featured on soundtracks with his saxophone performances.

Above: Wayne Shorter.

RETRO SWING

The 90s brought a much-needed revitalisation to jazz through a return of the conventional swing band. Retro swing reproduces the happy-go-lucky, swinging, bouncing feel of the 30s and 40s but with faster beat rhythms and electric instruments. Many of the retro swing bands also incorporate modern styles such as ska and punk into their repertoire alongside the traditional sounds of swing such as Glenn Miller's.

Although swing music had reappeared in modern music from time to time, it was not until the mid-90s that bands dedicated to playing strictly swing began to appear in California and were soon spreading out into the clubs.

EPILOGUE

Jazz is now over 100 years old and although styles, instrumentation and performance have evolved and changed over the passing years, the essence of jazz remains the same as it was at the time of its birth. Young jazz musicians are still inspired by the music that went before and continue to pick up and carry forward the blazing torch of jazz.

In the words of Louis Armstrong: "Musicians don't retire; they stop when there's no more music in them".

Above: Louis Armstrong.

INDEX

INDEX 125